I0414486

CALAMITY OF THE HEATHENS

By

Jimi Daniel Dillon

Why do the heathens rage and the people imagine…vain things?
Acts 4:25b

© 2002 by Jimi Daniel Dillon. All rights reserved.

No part of this book may be reproduced, stored in a retrieval system, or transmitted by any means, electronic, mechanical, photocopying, recording, or otherwise, without written permission from the author.

ISBN: 0-7596-7151-6

Library of Congress Control Number: 2002092081

This book is printed on acid free paper.

Printed in the United States of America
Bloomington, IN

1stBooks - rev. 05/06/02

DEDICATION

This book is dedicated to my wife, of American born, who is ignorant of my true nature. My early culture and conditioning produced this only partly understood husband of hers. She has had to contend with "this," she says. And to all my children, friends, and foes, whose searching questions to learn of my origin surface in benign conversations-conversations in which you dare not tell all for fear of disgust, distrust, personal humiliation to degrade, and ridicule. But now the whole story can be told and I hope it clarifies for them in my earlier reticence.

My heartfelt thanks to my dearly departed best friend, Moss. He surreptitiously, though subconsciously, saved the boy's life and his when they both, acting on childish and survival instincts, decided to move to Moss's uncle's ghetto shack. May his soul rest in peace.

Well, Billy Sticker*, you've always bulged your eyes when I told you; now bite your tongue! And don't choke on it!

Not only does the boy write for his West African ethnic groups that fall into this "heathenistic" category, but for all tribal groups around the "new world" who have been affected by the coming of the West to their shores or borders. I dedicated this book to them.

My special thanks to the National Geographic Society for its ceaseless efforts in trying to educate the rest of the world about the various smaller cultures and subcultures that time seems to have forgotten. *National Geographical* was instrumental in refreshing my memory while I toiled in telling this personal tragedy of my original "place in life" in the human kingdom.

SPECIAL NOTE:
The writer's name varied – in telling this personal tragedy

TABLE OF CONTENTS

PART I

PART II

PART III

PART IV

PART I

Jimi Daniel Dillon

Chapter 1

The Beginning

It happened one glowing evening as the sun was setting. Something was brewing in this tribal village of approximately fifteen huts. A boy's family hut stood on the Northeast corner of this West African village of Liberia. In the back of their hut stood the only orange tree of the entire village. It belonged to his family. There was a large cluster of banana trees also. Their shadow had dwindled awaiting the completion of the sunset. Late farmers hurried home to beat the dawn of nightfall.

The abrupt statement contrasted with the peacefulness of the falling night. "Lablekgahe (La-Blek-Gah), I want you to go to Monrovia with your cousin George Kekeh." The voice was devoid of emotion, as if the speaker were reciting a ritual in *Kpelle* (Pel-e), his tribal language. Lablekgahe was about 4 feet tall, thin weighing 60 pounds and pot-bellied. He stood very attentive for it was customary for a boy born in this bleak tribal society to pay attention to his parents and most elders of the village if he hoped to survive and grow to be a strong young man of the tribe. "I don't want you to be *ploutou*, like us," his father said. "I want you to go to Monrovia and go to school, so you can learn something. If you learn books, nobody will make a fool of you and enslave you like they are doing us here in Liberia.

This West African village of Liberia had a thriving brush and burn farming economy with strong family and community values and ties. At that time the village was full of healthy children and young people.

Villagers had a renewed hope of better life due to encroachment of Western culture, with Christian Missionaries coming to their borders. Due to the evils of recent wars very few people now live there, if not a ghost town today.

Ploutou was a form of slavery. Mandatory government farm labor that certain men of the villages were chosen at random to perform. They were expected to serve without a reasonable notice of their selection or knowledge of when the assignment would end. If the town chief and his immediate relatives did not like a person he could be sent almost every year.

Lablekgahe's father, a victim of the depression following World War II was considered *queh* (civilized) by most of the men of the village. The old man had lived in the city of Monrovia for approximately two years with a family when he was a boy. However, this setup did not work out and Lablekgahe's father went back to live in the village.

The old man's father had died before he was born and his mother died while he was still very young. He had learned to survive and work hard. During his city life, which was brief, he had learned a little broken English mixed with popular tribal expressions that had taken on some English meaning.

The villagers considered him educated enough to represent them at the government farm. While this was an honor, it meant that he received no pay for his labor while his family's affairs were left unattended.

Unfortunately, the same villagers did not like him enough to make him their town chief. It was for this reason the old man wanted his oldest son to go to Monrovia to school.

The old man was crossed-eyed in the left eye. He therefore spoke with his head tilted to the right. He stood 5 feet, 5 inches, leaning to his right when he spoke. He looked his son straight in the eyes and did not blink. His son had a slight smirk on his face. The old man's words left no room for argument. Because the boy had never been to a city before, the only image he could conjure up was George Kekeh, his distant cousin. Within the tribal society the inhabitants were distant related to almost everyone within that village and its environs. Although Cousin George is now deceased, the boy remembers that day very well.

Cousin George clean shaved, with his hair cut and most amazingly dressed in long pants and shoes stood right before his eyes, a sight little Lablegahe had been taught belonged to the *queh* (civilized) man. He instantly imagined that one day he too would be dressed up like his cousin. He too would have long pants, shirt, and shoes on his feet and a hair cut in which you could see the razor lining as was around George's head. The boy glanced back at his father, whose hair was cut with a crude, handmade razor knife that could not be used for a smooth shave. He decided city life might be enjoyable after all.

Chapter 2

The Journey That Seemed Endless

The next morning little Lablekgahe took a lukewarm bath with a pail of water his mother had prepared for him. This happened in the back of their hut. His father had built a roofless makeshift standing bath enclosure. He quickly threw the water over his back, face, arms and legs in this order and that was that. There was no towel or soap. Most people in the village of the 1940's and 1950's did not bathe with soap.

Lablekgahe's only possessions for the journey were his new Khaki shorts and a short-sleeved *Fanti* shirt. Fanti shirt is like a Hawaiian flower-patterned shirt. These clothes were kept at the bottom of his father's wooden trunk. All the good clothes were kept in one trunk or wooden valise or box and were worn only on important days such as death in the family, a Christmas season play, a ritual play or celebrating societal inductions and graduations. The meal before the uncertain journey was a bowl of rice covered with potato greens that had been cooked with red palm oil, a piece of dried monkey meat and some dried *bunny*. *Bunny* is a type of fish from the carp family. The meal was quickly eaten in the presence of the family, while the rest had to wait and eat separately from the boy, a sort of honor to him. Cousin George was also given something to eat for the long journey ahead.

Lablekgahe's mother was unhappy about his going away to the city for school, but she managed to hide her true feelings, simply saying "I hope nothing bad happens to my first son." His father tried consoling his wife saying, "nothing bad will happen to him, by the grace of god. Besides the country is now open with opportunities not like the old days during the war." Cousin George tried also to console her by saying, "Lablekgahe is going to be *queh* and then he'll come back as a big man." His father smiled and added, "he will be our redeemer someday! I know he will! What I failed in he'll conquer!"

On the day of their departure the rest of the family walked them to the edge of the village to the dusty road that led away from the village to the unpaved highway. His mother hugged him wishing him good luck trying to hold back her tears. Other siblings shook his hand, and then Cousin George shook everyone's hand and bid them goodbye.

The walk to civilization began one sunny morning in 1957. There was an assortment of wild birds flying through the jungle canopy above the foot road. A squirrel or more were seen jumping and climbing tree branches. The tall trees kept the sun off the walkers heads, although the long walk caused them to sweat. Cousin George, Lablekgahe and his father stopped at a brook once to drink fresh and free running water. The boy's father would accompany them as far as to the motor highway. He toted a *kinjah* on his back. A kinjah is a braided palm leaf elongated backpack that covers the entire back starting at the neck. It was full of foodstuffs; a five-gallon can of palm oil balanced on his head, as well as a white rooster tucked under his arm. These were commodities for his son to take to his new guardian and new home in the city. In a little over three hours they arrived at the motor road where he and Cousin George would get on a truck and ride for about three more hours to the capital city of Monrovia. Though the walk was exhausting, little Lablekgahe's eagerness to embrace civilization provided the energy he needed. He did not even feel much of the long and tedious walk although he was only about nine years old. Transportation was very scarce in the part of the country in those days. The boy's father could not wait to see them off, so he shook his hand, hugged him and handed him the white rooster for good luck. He started his journey back to the village before the darkness of evening crept up the narrow roadway. Wild animals and poisonous snakes were the main incentives to travel the wild, narrow road back to the village before it got too dark to see.

Chapter 3

Brawl in the Jungle, Western Style

As the boy watched his father walk away towards the village, he felt a little anxiety and sorrow. Cousin George told him they had a long time to wait for the truck that would take them to Monrovia, their ultimate destination. He told Lablekgahe that they would have to walk up the highway to visit some old acquaintances of his so he could learn how frequently passenger trucks traveled on that highway on a daily basis.

As the boy and Cousin George waked toward a small squared one-story zinc roof house on the roadside, Cousin George began to try to pry into the boy's history and find out if he was a fighter and how many boys in his village he had fought and whipped. As the boy invented stories of how he had fought and whipped other boys in his village, Cousin George just chuckled. The boy realized that this conversation was not in his best interest as he spotted two boys on the porch of the house they were heading towards.

The boy's heart began to beat faster when he remembered stories of how civilized boys were strong, how they could fight and how they had often beaten boys from the interior. He also surmised that George's conversation was about to lead to something. Something he said to the two boys on the porch didn't seem quite right. The bigger boy about Lablekgahe's size and age, said something like, "who me?" Pointing towards his own body and grinning, Cousin George nodded his head, and answered, "yes."

What followed was a superfluity of words from the stranger's mouth as he walked towards Lablekgahe with his fist balled up, but not close enough to touch him. Lablekgahe, who could not understand nor speak English, had already sensed aggression and he stood firm to defend himself if the stranger struck him. He could not reply to what he assumed were insults that the strange boy had leveled at him because he could not understand nor speak English, but he saw Cousin George laugh at whatever the boy had said to him. Lablekgahe looked the strange boy straight in the eyes until the boy walked away and back to the smaller boy on the house porch. Lablekgahe's fears quickly disappeared when the stranger failed to strike him first. He then walked away, but he did not soon forget this incident for he had heard that in Monrovia this type of encounter was common place.

Chapter 4

Lablekgahe's First Automobile Ride

Now that the encounter with the boys was over, Lablekgahe began to wonder when the truck would come. He had never ridden in a truck before. He had seen a few at the market grounds where he had gone with relatives to exchange goods, a barter system villagers participated in.

They heard the sound of an engine revving in high gear, climbing Gborker Hill, one of the highest elevations in that area of Bong County, Liberia. The truck finally stopped a little way past where they stood. George walked over and talked to the driver. Then he came back to their load beside the road.

Lablekgahe was excited that the truck had finally come. A man followed Cousin George to help them get their belongings and load them on the truck. The man's clothes were caked with dry red dust. He was unshaven and wore an old baseball cap backwards. His dusty, dirty bare feet reminded Lablekgahe that this man was commonly called a "carboy," meaning truck attendant.

The carboy's responsibilities included loading and unloading the truck and helping passengers get on and off the truck at various pick-up and drop-off points. He also fueled the truck, checked the oil and tire conditions and covered the open truck with a tarpaulin when it rained. He was like the driver's rear eyes and sometimes collected fares from some passengers who tried to claim, "I forgot to pay." That meant he had to chase quite a few who would have gotten away without paying their fares. The man helped Cousin George and the boy put their goods and belongings in the back of the truck. Then he gave Lableckgahe a big wide smile and said, "you goin' to Monrovia to be a big man, huh?" I tell you, you can learn book but ain't easy!"

The carboy ended his short oration, which was like a prophecy that could come true slowly. Lablekgahe remembered his father had said that he should go to Monrovia and "learn book." Cousin George had told his mother that her son was going to be *queh* (civilized) and educated and he would come back home to her as a big man. He considered the three valued opinions together and surmised "I'm going to learn book and I will be a big man so as to make my people happy."

He and Cousin George climbed into the truck. The carboy followed except that instead of climbing into the truck, he shut the tailgate, latched it together, and waited for the truck to take off. He then chased the truck, jumped, and grabbed the latched gate and clambered over it to get into the back of the truck. Lablekgahe sat firmly on the wooden bench along the side of the truck with feet, legs and knees together.

He grabbed a wooden rail with both hands on both sides of his body as though he was stretched on a cross except without the nails driven through his hands and feet. The railings that all passengers held onto were part of the truck's structure. Cousin George, who seemed always to be smirking, asked Lablekgahe if he was scared. The boy shook his head "no", trying hard to protect his manliness, a quality that was emphasized in his early tribal education and conditioning.

The six other passengers in the back of the truck were sitting opposite each other and rocked back and forth or swayed with the motion of the truck. They all looked at the boy when he nodded to mean that he was not afraid. It seemed to him that some were thinking, "but why is he lying?"

A few may have been thinking, "bless your heart, boy! Be strong!" but whatever they were thinking, Lablekgahe did not pay them much attention. He looked at Cousin George as though he was expecting a final command of what to do next. The words that came from Cousin George's mouth were, "Monrovia, here we come!" the experience of riding in the truck as it roared down the unpaved highway can only be described as like riding a roller coaster. The ride may have taken three hours, but to Lablekgahe it lasted forever!

The truck probably stopped to refuel before reaching Monrovia, but Lablekgahe did not even remember. He was too sick at his stomach from the diesel fumes. Also his head was spinning from the bumpy ride. When the truck finally arrived in the city, he threw up. Later he admitted to Cousin George that the fumes had made him sick all the way from their pickup point.

Chapter 5

The Beginning of a New Life

With a breath of a different air, not necessarily fresher than the one he was used to breathing back home in the West African jungle, Lablekgahe got off the truck. He looked himself over, as if to make sure he was still in one piece after the long, rough and nauseating ride he had experienced on the way to Monrovia.

Having been taught by tribal custom to "watch where you step," he looked down and for the first time he saw several paved car roads (streets for automobiles). He looked up, again relying on the tribal teaching of "watch where you are going." He noticed the high street lights and colorful traffic lights, for it was late in the evening. He could not relate these lights to anything he had seen before. Then it dawned on him that, yes, he was now in Monrovia. He was now in the civilized world. Certainly things would be new and strange to all of his senses.

Lablekgahe and Cousin George unloaded only the boy's belongings at a big brown-framed, two-story house. It stood on a corner of two streets in the heart of Monrovia. They met some young men in the big brown house, and Cousin George spoke English to them. The young men appeared guilty and smiled mildly at the boy. They did not shake the boy's hand as they did Cousin George. Cousin George told Lablekgahe "put your goods in the kitchen. He'll help you," pointing to one of the young men.

Cousin George told the boy that they were to meet his new mother (guardian) as were referred to over at George's house. George's mother (guardian) was a relative of Lablekgahe's mother. They got into a car of a friend of the mother George, and she took them to George's house. The boy had not yet learned of and about car riding. Everything seemed to be going in the opposite direction and very fast. At the stoplights everything looked different and so huge, compared to things and huts of his village. Only the giant forest trees beat most of the big buildings in the city to the best of his recollection.

The new society into which Lablekgahe was now about to be indoctrinated is a complex one. The society began with the arrival and settlement of a group of ex-slaves on this West African coast, later to be called Liberia. The name "Liberia" itself was derived from the Latin word "Liber", which means, "free". This group of ex-slaves and sons of ex-slaves who were freed in America immigrated to Africa, when the slave trade ended between 1800-1832. after their arrival they met the natives, some of whom may have been their relatives from whom they were snatched and sold into slavery. Others went north as far as Sierra Leone, Ghana (then known as the Gold Coast) and the Ivory Coast.

After the arrival of these ex-slaves and their sons, they married and inter-married with some of the natives. They bought lands a thousand percent below its true value, for the natives were not yet educated to the true value of their land. The new arrivals help build better living quarters, schools and churches.

They also showed the natives how to make simple gardens for growing vegetables and other foodstuffs. These natives that intermarried and intermingled with the ex-slaves and sons of "free men of color" were those who lived along the coast. There were vast numbers of other tribal groups and societies who lived far out in the hinterlands of that West African jungle. I, Lablekgahe, was an offspring of the Kpelle tripe. It was 1957 when Lablekgahe went to live in the city where the country had won her independence on July 24, 1847.

Liberia had her independence from the United States, which had colonized before July of 1847. Even now, a hundred years later, the economy was poor. The inhabitants still used the old method of "simple tools" farming rather than modern technology. This is the reason Lablekgahe's father had to go away to do *ploutou* work on government farms. The country's economy relied heavily on the United States for financial help as well as technical assistance and assistance in other areas such as education and building of roads and bridges.

Chapter 6

The New Relationship of Master-Servant

When the ex-slaves and children of the free men of color left the American plantations and returned to the West African coasts, they took with them the rudiment of slavery. Lablekgahe was soon to find this out firsthand when he and Cousin George met the boys master-guardian to be. The lady, as so she was, asked Cousin George,"what is his name?" referring to Lablekgahe. George replied, "his father call him Lablekgahe and everybody else call him Yankphin." "Well", she said, "I'm going to call him Daniel. Daniel in the lion's den." Lablekgahe looked at the lady with a puzzled expression. He glanced at Cousin George, who had a broad smile on his face. George rubbed his hand through the boy's hair and said, "your name is Daniel; that's your *queh*{civilized} name, you hear?" The boy nodded his head since he could not yet speak English. He knew to agree with everything he was told.

As people saw him nod his head to mean that he understood his new name, all faces lighted up with smiles as they repeated his name and he made rounds to shake the streched-out hands that welcomed him. It was a regular Sunday afternoon gathering of relatives and friends of the family at the house were Cousin George lived. This is where the boy's first introduction to this civilized society took place.

It suddenly dawned on little Lablekgahe that he had now entered civilization and that he had also lost his most important and inherent identity – his tribal names, including Nayhee – an affectionate name used only by his mother. In this little West African country names are important. For example Monrovia, the capital city, was named after James Monroe, President of the United States at the time to honor him. Some cities and townships were also named after the various presidents who came to power and other prominent men who were instrumental in the resettlements. Some helped the country get her independence as well as a place on the world map.

Though the country adopted a democratic form of government at its independence in July of 1847, it functioned as an anarchy. With little social reform, the country was ruled by dictators in principle and practice. The leaders preached democratic government in name only. The political, social and economic conditions of the country still do not reflect a democratic society. The leaders and their families had everything and the rest of the country suffered poverty in all areas.

Daniel who was formerly called Lablekgahe by his father, Yankphin by everybody else in his village, and Nayhee by his mother soon discovered that he had another name. If he did not respond to his name "Daniel", or did not move fast enough to do a task and especially if he did his chores sloppily, he heard his master-guardian scream, "boy, come here and scrub these pots and pans!" In his former home in the village, his mother and relatives had used the old clay pots or iron pots that did not need scrubbing for shine. This is why he did a poor job scrubbing the pots for the first time.

The new relationship consisted of a master-guardian, just like in the old American south. The master-guardian took in a child of an aborigine or a tribal family to be a servant. These native children, as they were called, were made basic house servants. The master-guardian was the son or daughter of an ex-slave whose forefathers were freed men of color. Most of the master-guardians had had some form of education in the Western or American cultures.

Even though some could not read or write, they spoke the Queen of England's language, English, and were familiar with the civilized way of living. The master-guardian's responsibilities to the native child included indoctrinating the child to the Western culture and the American way of life. The child was first taught how to speak English, though the grammar and the proper application of the language were not always accurate. In some homes, where the master-guardian was not adequately educated himself, the child often learned to speak broken English or to use colloquialisms. This was unfortunate. It hampered the child's progress of learning what was right and wrong grammatically. Secondly, when and if that child went to school at all, he or she could not function properly in class due to the lack of vocabulary of things in their common environment, especially those things that appear in the textbooks used to teach them. It is worthy to note that since Liberia was a former colony of the United States of America, the Liberian educational system was fashioned after that of the United States. Liberia even uses all American textbooks to date. The master-guardian was also responsible for the total well being of the native child he had taken into his home. The basic necessities of shelter, clothing, medical care, and food were included in the arrangement.

For most of these native children, the new role of servant was a traumatic experience. Their illiterate parents often did not know the educational level of some of these new master-guardians. Neither did the native parents know the social and psychological mentality of these master-guardians. Yet they entrusted their children into their care.

The problem of child abuse and child labor was high within the new class of master-guardians. A high percentage of the native children were ill cared for in terms of personal hygiene. They were allowed to go dirty for days, lacked proper clothing and sometimes had no shoes or a decent place to sleep. Most of the young native servants slept on floors and did not wash or change their garments often. Hence they were nicknamed "Dirty Joes." This nickname was used to humiliate further these unfortunate tribal youths. This was often the case when they got involved in a brawl or fight with another child of the civilized class or when they became mischievous or disrespectful to an adult.

The situation in reality was even more frustrating and sad for some of those African native children. Those who failed to transition to their new environment for any number of reasons or for no reason at all could be sent to their parents and face ridicule in their village for failing their peer group they had left behind. Some could not return to the master-guardian after they had been put out or had run away for fear of being abused, especially with a whip. Some had run away because the master-guardian had used them solely for the purpose of servitude and had neglected to send them to school. And those the master-guardian had labeled "bad" could not get a second chance to start all over again. Those children who went back to their parents in the village faced another obstacle. Some of their native parents became skeptical and unwilling to send them back to the previous master-guardian. Others were unwilling to trust their child and send him back to the city to a new master-guardian. The young people who had reached puberty generally got involved with someone of the opposite sex whom they had met during their transitioning stage. Some were willing to risk everything concerning their education rather than return to their respective villages. Some took the risk and found another master-guardian.

Those displaced native servants who could not find another master-guardian and who did not want to return to their tribal parents and villages became drifters around the city. They often banded together, forming a new societal class of the already existing "have-nots." They often stole, burglarized, and gambled on a daily basis to make a living. They slept in alleyways, in old abandoned shacks or on the open public beaches. Those who established themselves with a group often chose a partner or two and rented a room in an old ramshackled zinc house in the worst ghetto of Monrovia. Zinc is the sheet metal used chiefly for roofing. This particular subclass of displaced tribal children became permanently labeled "Grona Boys." The Grona Boys can be compared to those outcast British delinquent youths referred to as "Tedd Boys," in the 1960's and early 1970's.

Chapter 7

The Kitchen Boy Syndrome

Another dilemma of the tribal children who came from the interior into the city in search of a civilized way of life was the label of "kitchen boy." Most of the native boys who stayed in the city got branded with such a label because the daughters of the so-called upper class or the former ex-slaves and civilized master-guardians thought and perceived them as being inferior. This was partially due to the fact that these children, especially the boys, did indeed labor as house servants, scrubbing pots and pans and washing floors on their hands and knees. Their outward appearance usually showed the mark of their trade. They were dressed shabbily with the cheapest homemade clothing made in Japan or hand-me-downs from the children of their master-guardian. The lack of attention to them by their master-guardians and their lack of attention to their own personal well being and appearance was due to the overload of their responsibilities as servants showed on them. Some did not get their hair cut often and whenever it was cut, it was a crude home cut. The tribal servant children did not get the hygienic materials they needed for their personal upkeep such as soap, hair grease, deodorant, combs, and other needed items.

The young native or tribal servant's responsibilities were enormous, and it is no wonder that many became displaced, were put out, or ran away. While I cannot speak for every servant, I can faithfully speak for Daniel, formally called Lablekgahe, and many who ill-fitted that role. Daniel's master-guardian was a divorced female who had mostly grown children; two of those daughters and their families did not live in Monrovia. At first Daniel moved around a lot with his master-guardian she took turns visiting her children and their families. They lived far away from the capitol city. The small cities that Daniel's master-guardian visited were void of the big city modern conveniences. There were no plumbing facilities for running water, and no gas or electric stoves for cooking. In those small cities Daniel had to live with his master-guardian in the early stages of his indoctrination into the so-called civilized society without modern necessities. This meant that Daniel had to draw water from the well that was quite a ways from the small semi-modern house they lived in. Daniel had to carry a pail of water sitting on his head from the well to the house and pour it into a 100-gallon drum or barrel until it was full. He fetched wood and also had to make the fire on the open hearth or in the old wood burning stove each morning. Often it was the very first thing he did after he woke up in the mornings. He then had to put water on the fire for the bath of his master-guardian as well as the rest of the family. The house consisted of the master-guardian's married daughter, her husband, and their three children. Daniel often times had to go and fetch wood from the surrounding brush field if any could be found or go to the market grounds and buy some wood to keep the fire alive until all had taken their baths.

Daniel also had to cut or split the wood so that it would fit on the open hearth or fit into the old cast iron wood-burning stove. Unfortunately Daniel was too young to do this particular chore; he was a skinny eight-to-ten year old boy. When Daniel would stop throwing the axe into the log to catch his feeble breath, he would often wonder about what his father had told him about not wanting him to be a *ploutou* or work free for the government. He would wonder, too, if this new relationship of master-guardian to servant was not the same as *ploutou*. But Daniel persevered, believing that his father understood and knew what was best for him or else he would not have sent him off to a total stranger to help him get his education.

It was irrelevant to Daniel that in his new Liberian society the government was far behind in modernization of the city, especially the small cities such as the one Daniel lived in with his new master-guardian. The house were they lived was equipped with a small oil-burning electric generator. Fortunately there was at least minimal electricity although they experienced frequent nights of blackout when the machine broke down or ran out of fuel oil.

This one-story house with three bedrooms had a regular bathtub but no running water. It was square with zinc sheet roofing. The kitchen was built outside in the back of the house. Daniel also had to keep the house clean, mainly sweeping the floors plus washing the bathroom and kitchen floors daily. He usually washed the dishes, and scrubbed the pots and pans after each dinner. He often times ran errands to the small corner store or took a message across town to his master-guardian's relative, friend or fiancée. There were no telephones in many cities in those days.

One of the roles that upset young Daniel was called the "pu-pu boy" syndrome, or better known as the "shit pot carrier." At this early stage of Daniel's indoctrination into civilized society, he learned that at night his master-guardians used a special pail or bucket with a top for waste matters. Each morning he had to empty this pail outside into the non-modern toilet or "W.C.," {water closet}, as it was commonly called. He also had to wash this infamous pail or bucket inside and out and put it away for the next night. This was also true for the rest of the citizens of that small city because there were no modern plumbing facilities. Even in the daytime, especially when someone had diarrhea, Daniel's potty run was doubly humiliating. He had to empty that pail day and night. The latrine was also called the *cheemun*; hence the boy was also called "cheemun boy" as a derogatory term.

Chapter 8

Daniel's Dilemma

Daniel and other house servants to the children of the master-guardian were stepchildren, or so were referred to by the master-guardian. I believe it helped ease their minds of the guilt that they were informally enslaving other people's children, just like their fathers and forefathers were enslaved by the great yet infamous southern plantation owners of America. The masters taught their children to regard tribal children and servants as their stepbrothers and sisters. That way the subject of servitude could grow subtle and unpronounced in the minds of their children and younger generation, for even the masters themselves were emotionally trying to bury and forget the years of slavery that their fathers and forefathers were once subjected to. After all, it was to escape physical, mental and emotional trauma of slavery that these freed men of color had left the American shores to form the country of Liberia.

In addition to all the humiliating chores Daniel had to perform, his master-guardian's daughter or his stepsister burdened him with yet other dehumanizing name. Her infamous, yet keen perception was derived from another mark of the "trade" that appeared on Daniel and that was already haunting him. Daniel had toted or carried water, wood, and other chore-related goods on his head so much and so long that the top center of his head had grown bald. The master's daughter nicknamed him "kpola head" (pronounced "polar head"), signifying a bald head. Baldness was looked down upon as a sign of extreme poverty, and implied someone who was unlearned in this Liberian society. The name-calling produced laughter by those in the immediate environment especially peer group. The mockery sunk Daniel's already low self-esteem.

The name calling to put down or degrade, the beatings for little or nothing stemmed from their slave master's ignorance, ignorance that these behaviors would leave permanent scares-mental, physical, and spiritual. Perhaps the slave masters had learned this behavior from the slavery under which their forefathers were brought up. Those were the ways to train up a child; the slave masters merely copied them. Only recently have psychologists and sociologists scolded the human society, warning that beatings, scolding, and name-calling can ruin the child. Such children can become abusive children or adults themselves. Indeed it is true. The boy, once he was a parent, often times caught himself punishing his children in like manner and would quickly stop and regret what he had done.

The effects of the harsh punishment did not stop when he left his master-servant relationship. When the boy, now and adult, was in West Africa visiting kin folks after having lived in the United States, my niece had stolen something for which she was being whipped severely to discourage her from repeating the act. She cried to the boy for help to save her from her mother's viscous whip that cut her across the back, legs, and arms. The boy (now an adult) jumped in the midst of the scene and caught a few of the lashes on his arms and sensitive areas. The melee was hardly over when the boy turned to hide his face, for tears had welled up in his eyes and were about to trickle down his cheek. He quickly walked away into his room, overpowered by memories and fighting desperately to avoid being seen crying. That would embarrass him very much for the boy, now a fully grown man, had just arrived from the United States, the richest country in the Western world, a world where people were suppose to have it together.

On this trip the boy's relatives sat around to talk to him, admire him, and tell him of some of their hardships, trials, and tribulations. One difficulty was that the country had been at war for a long time. This was one reason the young girl had tried to steal a little money to purchase something to eat. From that moment on, the boy gave that niece some of whatever he was eating. The boy also told the child after the beating that whenever she was hungry, she should come and ask him for food or money to buy something to eat.

The boy can simply ask that you have pity on the angry mother. Ordinarily this terrible beating of her child would not have happened. She was ignorant of the effects this would have on her child both present and future scars that would be left, both physically and mentally. Though in today's society it would be considered a case of child abuse, the mother's act stemmed from cultural conditioning that is still practiced today, especially in that part of the world.

During Daniel's first two to three years in "civilization," he traveled a lot with his first master. He rode in the back of an open truck. Master sat in the front seat with the driver. The roads were unpaved; therefore his hair was mostly reddish, a direct result of red clay dust that blew on them in the open back end. His raggedy shorts and short-sleeve hand me down shirt was usually caked with dust during those trips.

At night carboy would pull down and cover the back of the truck with a tarp to protect the merchandise and keep rear passengers warm from the forest winds. The carboy usually slept in the back at night to protect goods on board. When the truck was empty, he normally would room with someone such as a friend or relative. The boy spent some time with his master on a farm called Maybay Farm. How long they were on this farm is uncertain. He had not yet learned to measure time in terms of minutes, hours, dates, day, or years. On the farm other servants teased him about not knowing how to speak English, but also helped him learn some names of things and English words. He remembers Pewee, a cross-eyed servant. There was also a beautiful, shy servant girl, but he does not remember her name.

Daniel and his master later moved to a small city called Ganta. There the boy's role as a servant began to take a definite shape. Here in Ganta, the well was close by. It was in the back of the three-bedroom house. Half a drum or fifty-gallon barrel had to be filled up with water each day. It sat in the unfinished kitchen with no appliances. There, Daniel made the fire and heated the water for the master's bath. There was more than one master at this time.

He helped the master's child and two grandchildren get dressed and the parents dropped them off at school. It was a mission school. There was no school bus system in those days. When the children came from school, they each had small, but different needs. The boy served them all. The two male grandchildren of the master learned to play with Daniel and he liked that a lot. The older of the two boys was very liberal-minded. He even shared secrets with Daniel form time to time.

Even kids sexual secrets were shared over the years to come especially secrets of the girls he like, those he brushed against in school with the intent to "feel on her body." Daniel had very few secrets to confide to the master's oldest grandson. One he remembered was when he was very little that a bigger girl of the village had set him on her lap. She, being in heat, had taken his little "worm" and tried to put it into "her hook." This happened on Daniel's first fishing trip with the other village kids. He told how he was caught behind a hut. He and a little girl were standing against the dubbed mud wall of a hut. They were trying to do "bad things," a common name for kiddies' sexual acts in West Africa. This was especially so in the small cities, towns, and villages.

The boy told how the year before he came to Monrovia he got caught with and older girl. She had been molesting him for about three days early in the morning when he went out to urinate near the banana bushes on the outskirts of his village. The girl would be bathing in the makeshift open-topped outdoor bath cage. She would call the boy inside, take his little worm, and put it into her steamy "fish." The boy had not yet developed "sexual senses" and did not know what was going on. He went along with it though, just out of curiosity. Her "char glowing pink," like that of a fully burning coal on a hearth, turned little Daniel on even then.

After approximately a year in Ganta, the master and Daniel moved to Saniquellie, a city further into the interior. The master had a foster sister living and working there. The master was hired to work in the same hospital as her sister. Her foster sister was powerful and influential. That is how the master got this job, Daniel learned. Saniquellie was a larger city in size and population than Ganta. It had an airstrip, though it was unpaved. On Sunday afternoons the boy would go watch the single-engine planes land with propeller on their front tip, they made so much dust that Daniel did not see the pilots or occupants exit and go into the field house.

Since the boy did not yet speak English, he did not go to school yet. A Muslim family's son befriended him. The Muslim boy, older than Daniel, would push him around or punk him from time to time. He would also play with him off and on. The Muslim boy did not like school at all and did not go either. On late Sunday afternoons he would take Daniel swimming in a freestanding pond, not far from where they lived. The pond overflowed its' bank when it rained. It was partially muddy and full of algae and wild lilies.

The city was run by a commissioner, a very big, handsome, and quiet-looking man. He lived in a big, beautiful compound. Daniel remembers. The compound had a cluster of five small houses attached together in a row. Corner houses had elevated roofs above the three buildings between them. Cement was expensive and hard to find in those days, therefore the walls were made of clay blocks. And plastered with same giving them a semi rough look. The zinc sheet metal roofs were shining in the sun. The compound enclosure fence was higher in the back toward the forest and lower in the front. Mango trees littered the yard both front and back. It was situated several yards from the dusty highway and away from the main city-line, although within ears and eyes reach. He was sent there often to take notes to the commissioner's house from the master's foster sister also a second master to Daniel in the same household. Daniel also befriended a bigger boy on the commissioner's compound. He was very nice and talkative. There were several mango trees on the compound and Daniel and the compound boy would pick some and eat them.

Chapter 9

The Servants of Saniquellie

In Saniquellie City, J.W. Green had three other servants. Daniel was the fourth servant and also the youngest. J.W. Green was Daniel's master's foster sister. She was in essence Daniel's second master.

The two grown male servants pushed around Daniel, teased and laughed at him. They laughed because Daniel could not yet speak English well. He could not understand orders because he had not learned the names of certain things. He did the wood fetching, stove lighting, and cleaning of the ashes. He was also the water toter, filling the barrels daily.

One of the male servants was responsible for the personal upkeep of J.W.-getting her clothes ready for work, her bathroom cleaning and preparing her bath water as well as keeping the house clean. The second male servant did important errands, washed the master's clothes, ironed, and kept track of needed items and grocery shopping.

The single female servant did J. W's hair, personal female hygiene care, and other affairs Daniel was too small to understand. It was once rumored that the second grown male servant was having an affair with Bee, the female servant, and she was let go. Daniel suspected that J. W. wanted this second male servant as her house lover. He was tall, dark, and handsome with a bright beautiful smile. His name was "T" a shortcut for his first name.

The price and sacrifices for education are worth their weight in gold. And the boy was about to begin paying that price and begin the ritual of the sacrifices. Daniel started school in the late summer of 1958. The Saniquellie Public School allowed enrollment of even a servant like Daniel who could barely understand and speak English. The boy remembers that during his first few months of schooling he was confused. Having already learned some of his ABC's at home, he dealt with three small books. The books, approximately 10 ½" X 8" in size, had probably four to six chapters. They were called "My Blue Story Book", "My Green Story Book", and "My Red Story Book." The boy does not remember if they were in this order. Perhaps the word "little" preceded each color in the three titles of his beginning books.

On the first day of class the older black lady with light gray hair and a thin build gave him a note to hand to his master. It said to send money by Daniel for books. The teacher said it was a requirement, as if the boy knew what the word *requirement* meant then. He looked at the teacher with wide eyes and mouth open as though he wanted to ask her, "what in the world is a *requirement*?" But since he could hardly speak English, he could never ask such a question. For one thing, he could never remember the pronunciation nor the spelling or meaning of requirement. He took the note home to his master. She in turn put some change in an envelope, sealed it, and gave it to the boy. "You better not lose it, boy, and give it to the teacher," his master shouted.

The boy began school in the afternoon session, which ran from approximately 1:30p.m. to 5:00p.m. Most servants attended afternoon school. They had to perform most of their chores in the morning before going to school. Daniel had to walk to school. It was a "foot" made road through a field once used for growing ground peas (peanuts). It was irregular with steep patches of small hills. About halfway to the school on this back road, there was a big rock under a large but sparsely leafed tree. There, Daniel stopped and sat on the rock to catch his breath before reaching school. He could not yet form an opinion about whether he liked or disliked school. He had just gotten there and did not know what it all entailed. He remembers hearing the other children read out loud, standing before the teacher and the class. But for him, he had not reached that stage yet.

The class had homemade benches, placed in rows as in a church, but these wooden benches were shorter. They seated about five small kids each. There were four rows of benches. All Daniel remembers of his first class is the vivid colors of his three new books. He also remembers the pictures of *kwe-kowleh* [white people] and their beautiful houses with pretty yards and flowers. There were also pictures of cars in the books, but he does not remember what kind. The boy thinks some were convertibles. The first school experience lasted about a quarter (three months) of that summer year.

Chapter 10

Love and Romance in Saniquellie

With its heartache and deceits, romance blossoms around the world. It flickered in and out of the boy's life while he was growing up. His first romantic interest was a beautiful nurse. Nicknamed *Mo*, she often consoled the boy who was teased often by J. W. 's two grown male servants. He was teased because he had knocked knees. Needless to say, the condition developed as a result of scrubbing wooden and tile floors on his knees from a young age to his early teens.

Mo faced a dilemma. She dated one of the most powerful men in all of Liberia, the vice president. You would think a man of his status and class would know how to treat a lady lover, especially for the sake of his position in the government. He was married legally and was also suppose to be a man of God, a preacher. But most of the times he visited Mo, she would come out of her room crying. She tried hard to conceal her tears, but the boy knew better. He too, had shed many tears from mild home whippings, to sibling rivalry that escalated to fighting over the simple things of life most commonly food or when he felt cheated. Mo's tears could have meant only two things from the boy's point of view: exhilaration from sexual orgies between the two, or violence. The boy swears he heard beatings and screaming at times of the man's visits to Mo. The boy knew Mo's voice and could tell she was creaming from fear or pain and that he knew well. But the boy's worst beatings had not come yet.

Mo lived in the house where the boy's master lived with her foster sister, J. W. It was only a short stay on an irregular basis. The boy believes that the powerful J. W. sent for Mo to spend the weekends in order for the vice president to have an affair with her. These disturbing acts happened off and on until the boy and his master returned to Monrovia from Sanquellie.

A second living arrangement was with another female friend of the boy's master. She was Jamaican-born, American-educated and beautiful. She was cultured and compassionate. She reared a Bassa boy (a boy from another Liberian tribe) named Lafonte. He had everything a king's son could want, but he did not have a brain. He had flunked in early elementary school so many times that Lablekgahe from the jungle village, surpassed him in school. At the beginning Lafonte laughed at the boy's English. He would say, "Lafonte ma sayeh_da me_da you," meaning, "Lafonte. Ma says it's for me and you." Lafonte was instrumental in teaching the boy his first broken English phrase, "Ma say it's for me and for you." This happened when food was divided. Food for the boy and Lafonte was put in one bowl to eat. The boy brought the food to

Lafonte and was trying to say it was for both of them. Lafonte got a good laugh at the boy everyday.

After returning to Monrovia, and living with Lafonte and his master in about 1958, the boy and his master moved in with the master's second grown daughter and family. This ghetto suburb was known as *New Kru Town*. This was the same family they had stayed with in Ganta. The master's youngest daughter, Miss E, and her two grandsons began attending private grade school. In Ganta, they were in beginner's school. The boy's school life, which was brief in Saniquellie, was interrupted since there was no public school close by in this shanty suburb of Monrovia. The children were driven to school as their parents were on their way to work. They stayed until their parents got off work and picked them up. The boy did not go to school again for about a year or so. By this time he could understand and speak English better. He even attended Sunday school along with his master's daughter and two grandsons. He did not know what Christianity was all about, but he liked the attention from the missionary lady and the gathering while singing.

In New Kru Town the boy's eyes bulged with wonder when he first saw the electric light in the house. His curiosity drove him wild. One day when no one else was around, he decided to investigate further. He wondered whether electricity give out heat as did lanterns or fireplaces when they glowed in his jungle village. With total ignorance of the eminent danger the boy decided to do his own test. He took from the hearth a metal rod used to stir the fireplace. He stood on a chair for additional height and stuck the rod into the bulb socket. With a blasting shock, a lightning bolt went all through his body. He quickly dropped the rod and jumped off the chair with hands and body trembling. His knees were weak from the shock. He finally concluded that whether electricity gave out heat as did lanterns and fire, it was something he would not ever mess with again as long as he lived.

Another thing that fascinated the boy was seeing water flowing out of a piece of iron pipe as he later came to know them. Water was something that he many times had to fetch and tote in buckets or pails on his head for several hundred yards, whether it was on the farm or to the hut in the village. And now he could actually see it being turned on and off right before his very eyes. "Whoa!" the boy exclaimed, as he was really amazed.

Here in the shanty town lived some white diplomats. Their houses were fenced in near the unpaved one-lane street. One of those white men, the boy believes was a German. He owned a big dog-the size of a full-grown deer. He now knows it to be a German Shepard. Bi-weekly, as if it were ceremonial, he would bring his dog out, unleash it, and let it attack one of the pigs of a local owner. The dog would shake the pig almost to death. Holding the pig at its throat the dog would foam at its mouth until the pig bled profusely. When the pig was beginning to weaken, almost as if to die, the master would call off his dog. By this time, the rest of the herd of swine had run off to hide.

Probably this dog master was not just out by chance to exercise his dog and the pigs happened to be there by chance, on which he let loose his dog for exercising. The boy believes this so-called diplomat was a bloodthirsty sadist. By the way, the boy never saw any females in the environs of the house or yard. If an animal rightist could acquire the archives and pictures of foreign diplomats living and working in Liberia between the late 50's and early 60's, the boy believes he could pick him out from a lineup. He would support the animal rights organization to charge him withl cruelty to animals. He believes the diplomat would have allowed his dog to maul the boy, like those helpless pigs had he known that the boy was illiterate and could not speak English very well to report him to the authorities.

By late 1958 the boy moved with his master again to yet another suburb of Monrovia, again in J. W. 's house. This concrete block house with a zinc roof also had running water in the bathroom only. The boy filled up the used and empty pig feet barrel that sat in the far corner of the kitchen from the bathroom faucet. He used a bucket every morning and evening to do this chore. At least it was better than going to the well to draw water and walking several tiring trips with a bucket on his head.

The boy's most vivid memory about this residence was the cook. Since servant T had been put out, J. W. had hired a cook. Though Jimmy could not read or write he was a good cook. Jimmy had a partially broken right index finger. It resembled that of a professional one-finger keypunch operator of a typewriter or computer. It was curved and bent at the last joint. He used it mostly when he wanted to get his point across, when he wanted to convince you that he was telling the truth, or as a warning tool pointing in your face. J. W.'s other male servant nick-named him "hook Jimmy" because the finger looked like a hook. It was smaller than the rest of his fingers. We all got a laugh out of that name. He was most jovial, not insulted at all.

By the end of the year J. W. had gotten a big promotion. She also got a big pretty house in the heart of the city very near where she worked. This house was modern two-story concrete home. It had tile flooring and a sheet-metal roof. Outside it was painted green and square in structure with glass windows. The boy's master also got a job at this big government facility through J. W.'s influence and pull. This was the boy's first impression of civilized work and professionalism. J. W. was considered a hell raiser on the job. On occasion the boy saw and heard her scream at some of the people who worked under her. She was a go-getter and got things done her way most of the time. He also saw his master at work. Though quiet-natured, she too, screamed, though in a lower tone than J. W. at the three men who worked under her. She was an assistant supervisor and didn't seem to care that loading and unloading a truck by hand was not an easy task for those three.

Chapter 11

Sex Den in the House

J. W. had a grown son named LaChelles. He had grown up and lived in America from his teens to his forties. LaChelles loved young women. On a long visit home to Liberia, J. W. put him in a downstairs northern room that overlooked the Atlantic Ocean. It also overlooked a shanty cluster of old, used zinc houses. While overlooking this shanty town to check out the ocean view, LaChelles spotted a beautiful "Kru" tribal girl resident. He hurriedly called Daniel and sent him to call the girl. Daniel escorted the girl to LaChelles's room. They may have stayed in there for an hour or so, but to the boy, it seemed like all day. Because of his curiosity and the fact that he was developing sexual senses, he kept vigilance at the door of LaChelle.

When the door opened, the room filled with smoke, smoke of a strange cigarette. On occasion the boy was sent to a certain house with money to buy a small wrapping of this kind of cigarette. The smoke in the room sometimes made the boy sick at his stomach. He was called to clean the room of beer bottles and cigarette ashes from trays or the marbled floor. He also had to make up the bed. After this girl started coming to LaChelles's house regularly, she became the buyer/pickup person of this strange cigarette. The boy later found out that the strange cigarette was grass, marijuana, or African guanta. No wonder LaChelles's eyes were always red and the boy thought that he had an eye problem or was suffering from lack of sleep each and everyday. This rendezvous continued the entire summer. LaChelles finally returned to the United States.

At the same time that LaChelles's rendezvous was going on, Dodo, one of the three men working under Daniel's master had his going also. He was from the Bassa tribe and would have a new Bassa girl stop by the house every morning. This happened when LaChelles was gone out or had spent the night out. Other times Dodo would have the girls stop by his place of business. He would walk them over the one block from work to the house. He would use LaChelles's cold marble floor to do his thing. How does the boy know what went on in that room? He became curious enough to start peeping through the keyhole. He could see Dodo's naked butt pounce, rise, and fall. Sometimes it went in a circular motion, at which time the boy heard moaning and groaning sounds. There were other times some of the girls would say "ma nee, Dodo, ma nee." The boy later learned that the Bassa tribal word meant, "Leave me alone or stop." In approximately six months, the boy learned that Dodo got fired for stealing something from J. W., the master-guardian.

J.W. had another servant named JB. She treated him as if he were her own son. He was very smart and attended one of the two best private schools in the whole country and made good grades. He had a secret affair with one of the master's daughters. The boy went after them to check on their aftermath, so he knows what he's talking about. JB also had another girl named Athero. She was crazy about JB. Actually JB did not care whether she lived or died; he only wanted her for sex. She repeatedly fussed at him for not visiting her. Whenever she came over, usually at night, JB would put her on the table and pounce on her. She would wail, moan, and groan, calling out his name. Daniel would be lying down in a corner on his mat for bed and pretending to be asleep. Other times JB would send him on an errand so as to have privacy.

But the boy would run fast as he could so as to get back and try to get a sound view of the action. He rarely succeeded at these times, as these errands were purposely planned to prevent his return while bodies were in motion.

PART II

Jimi Daniel Dillon

Chapter 12

I'll have your Birthright Too

For whatever reason masters changed the name of native children, Daniel can't really say. His guess is that their names were changed for selfish reasons. Perhaps it was so the children of the natives could blend into their new "Americo-Liberian" society. They, Americo-Liberians, and their forefather's names were changed after their arrival in the new world, or at the plantations of the South. They perhaps felt too, that they had the right and the upper hand to do the same to the young native servants. Or perhaps they felt that they were too educated to fool with such names as Lablekgahe and Yakpakwoloh. The boy does not know for sure their reasons, yet Daniel still remembers that they often made jokes of their original African and aborigines names.

In the early eighties, one of Daniel's younger brothers wrote to him for financial help. He was about to graduate from high school in Liberia. What puzzled the boy is that he could not remember a brother called Nelson. So who was Nelson Kekulah? Kekulah was the middle name of one brother. As the boy wondered, it suddenly dawned on him that the Americo-Liberian family with whom this boy was raised by had done it again. Through subtle ridicule of his tribal name, Kekulah, they had changed or caused him to change his name to Nelson. He too had finally been brainwashed to think that his native tribal name of Kekulah, with which he was born, did not sound right. And perhaps would not fit into the Liberian modern society.

For the boy, he always knew that one-day he would regain his rightful and prominent first name and it was that of his father. In the tribal society, the boy child had the right to take his father's first name. This was especially true if he was the first boy child, sort of like a "junior."

Daniel realized and remembered that while he was just a little boy, growing up in the village, people called him "Jimi-Lon", meaning "little Jimi" or "son of Jimi." He kept this thought intact in the back of his mind. He knew that one day; he too would be called Jimmy. His thought and dream became a reality, when he finally graduated from high school. He used the given name Daniel from his first master, sneaked in a middle name, Jimi, and then used Dillon, his master's last name.

Whether the Liberian-born children licked their food bowls with their fingers and tongues (they had no spoons), or wore bumba and straw skirts, they were and are still a people. They too are a people with firmly fixed identities, ethnically diverse, fiercely independent and egalitarian in spirit and instinct. A name change was not necessary and did not mean "a hill of beans." We were all Liberians.

The boy was born with the first name, "Yank-Pund." The name describes the walk of a shrimp or crawfish. According to the boy's mother, he was sickly and shriveled physically. Therefore, when he walked, he resembled the walking of a shrimp or crawfish. In fact, he was so sickly that his mother simply called him "Nayeh", pronounced as "Nate". It simply means "you," but more like "ah," in a sense. She later told how she did not think he would survive; hence a proper name was not necessary at the beginning of his life. On the contrary, based on fatherly faith, his dad named him Lablekgahe. The Gisse tribal name simply means "little tall man." His dad believed the boy would grow up skinny, but tall.

Separation Anxiety

It is said "absenteeism makes the heart grow fonder," but in Daniel's case it almost proved disastrous when he did not see much of Cousin George in the first three years of his breaking into civilized society. It was now the year 1959 and the boy Daniel had seen Cousin George for the last time before he left town for a job up country. He did not even let Daniel know of his plans, nor did he bid Daniel goodbye. Daniel found out through a second hand source as the news made him sad and even a little nervous.

It was perhaps in this same year that Daniel started the first grade. His second public school was called Bassa Community School. The boy had to walk to this afternoon school. It took him about one and a half hours one way. The boy had now gotten use to walking long distances. He went to the marketplace each morning to buy daily foodstuffs to be cooked. He also had to wash pots and pans and clean up the kitchen, before going to school. He did not mind the long walk and resultant sweaty body and clothing. He was excited that he had once again begun his schooling. He remembered his father's instructions "to go to the city and learn books," so he would not have to be a *plotou* as his father and kinfolks were. The boy had developed the ability to listen and learn, a quality he had developed in his early days in his tribal village.

His greatest feat in this first grade class was the creation of the "best scrapbook of the class for that year." He got a standing ovation from his classmates, a handshake from his teacher, and a one hundred percent on his one page book inside cover. Thanks to the company that made tomato juice, tomato paste, and mixed vegetable labels in those days. The vivid pictures on them made the boy's scrapbook come alive.

At the end of the school year Daniel passed to the second grade, but not before getting a whipping because another boy, Daniel Harris, had switched his report card and left his in Daniel's notebook. This happened when Daniel went to the bathroom. When he got home, his master inquired about his report card, not realizing it was Daniel Harris's card. It was a passing card, but mostly low grades. His master thought he had intentionally changed his name to Daniel Harris, so he got a beating and went back to the schoolhouse the next day. He told the teacher what had happened. The teacher sent to the house of Daniel Harris and got the right cards to the proper owners. She wrote a letter to Daniel Dillon's master explaining about the mix-up. The boy was left in peace for a short while after this incident.

Daniel started his third public school in approximately 1960. He was now beginning the second grade. His new school, Daniel E. Howard, was thirty to forty-five minutes closer than the former school. On occasion he dropped off errand items to his master on his way to school. She worked on one of the three routes Daniel could take to his new school.

At times he would hurriedly complete his chores so he could stop and admire the executive mansion and the soldiers who guarded it. The mansion was a three story colonial house with several windows on each level. It was painted white, with a beautiful manicured garden in front and back. The soldiers wore khaki uniforms from the United States army, with red beret and shoulder patches as well as black boots. They carried rifles at their side as they guarded the mansion.

By now Daniel had befriended Moss, another young male servant of his crowd. He also went to school with Moss who had just started the first grade. Moss lived with the rich family, from whom J.W. rented the beautiful house in which they lived. This rich family had eight servants at the time Daniel and his masters moved into their leased house on the compound of the rich family.

Daniel also began to learn another lesson that would last forever. Since he was an errand runner for the whole house, he bought cigarettes and liquor just to name a few vices. A distant nephew of J.W., Lou, moved into the home. From Niger, he was a typical playboy, but very secretive about his girls. In fact he did not disrespect J.W.'s house by bringing them there. Instead he slept out, when he went out from time to time.

Apart from being a heavy smoker and make Daniel's errands more frequent, he had a love affair with liquor called Guinness Stout. At that time the liquor was bottled and distributed in most of West Africa. That made it affordable and "Lou" drank a lot of it. He then changed his strategy. Instead of sending Daniel to buy the brew, he began to take the boy along. Daniel believes it was a strategy for Lou to tell women "No, I have the boy along with me." Women and girls were always chasing after him. He was suave, curly haired and brown-skinned, with the brown eyes that could pierce most women. He also had a sly smile and a British/French accent just about stopped most women in their tracks. But Lou had a hidden agenda also for taking Daniel to the popular neighborhood shopping and drinking hangout.

He and J.B. found out that the boy liked the dark brew after Lou had let the boy take one too many tastes. He and J. B. had joked about how he was going to get Daniel drunk. He got a great laugh out of seeing the boy stumble or stagger. He was surprised that Daniel vomited the first night on their way home. The second weekend, Daniel sat in a corner sleeping and nodding his head. After that, Lou told J. B. that the boy was now a drinking fish. He could drink up to two bottles a night and was able to walk with Lou home. He was surprised. The boy learned to say "No" after that, meaning he was not going anymore.

Chapter 13

High Play for Acceptance

In the servant's roles and the battle to thrive in the so-called Americo-Liberian society, servants oftentimes play high or play along with their master's games. For love or acceptance by master's children they played, or to be accepted by the children of their master's peers they played along with whatever games they were offered.

When Daniel was in the third grade, he was set up with a girl. One of his master's daughters (he would rather call his foster sister,) did the setting up. The unknown fiancé Kay-Jay, was the daughter of an educated and middle-class aborigine. The joke on Kay-Jay almost backfired. Kay-Jay would have fallen in love with Daniel, if several conditions had been different. First Daniel did not attend one of the schools of choice of the elite. There were five or perhaps six only. Secondly, Daniel was not wearing the uniform of one of those schools. Daniel was not in the right grade, and finally his hair had been cut crudely and unlined, a distinct sign of a houseboy or servant.

Daniel's foster sister in the sixth grade wrote a letter to Kay-Jay in Daniel's name. She stated that Daniel was deeply in love with Kay-Jay. She told Kay-Jay in the letter that Daniel was in the sixth grade, and that Daniel would meet her on Parade Day. Parade Day was probably July 24th.

That is considered Liberia's Independence Day by the Americo-Liberians. Daniel's foster sister also told him of Kay-Jay, while he was washing some clothes outside their house. She had a beautiful laugh, with natural white teeth. Though his young master had tricked Kay-Jay into believing that Daniel was in love with her and had written the letter, he agreed to go along with the plan.

On Parade Day, Daniel's foster sister brought Kay-Jay to about five full steps from where his school was dismissing from parade formation. She waited until Daniel walked away from the rest of the group line he was in. About ten steps away from the crowd, she demanded, "did you write me this letter?" There was anger and disappointment in her face and voice as she looked at me.

"Why did you lie about the school you go to", she continued, "are you really in the sixth grade?" Daniel slowed, then stopped walking. He looked at Kay-Jay and answered "No."

"But why did you say these things that are not true in your letter?" she asked. "You really did not write this letter, did you? It was your sister who wrote it, right?"

"Yes, but I told her to write it for me," lied Daniel. "We can be only friends," Kay-Jay told Daniel hurriedly. Then she looked at Daniel and said good-bye.

There was no smile on her face. Kay-Jay walked back to her friends, slowly walking down the street. A few years ago the boy heard that Kay-Jay had a great big wedding and in less than three years the marriage dissolved.

This new class of servants/masters were a hush, hush business. No master/guardian went around boasting about his or her boy servant. In those days, most servants carried their master's last name in school. Most servants were noticeable only by their half-dressed appearance. Usually the boys wore homemade elastic waistband shorts with matching shirt or plain T-shirt or round neck shirts. Most young servants did not wear anything on their feet, except on holidays. A very few got that luxury even then for those who were fortunate to wear good clothes, that is, long pants and shoes. For others they received hand-me-downs from the master's children.

The division between servant and master's family was almost always apparent in one form or another. Differences in dress were one, public school for most of the servants versus private schools for the master's children was another. Most servants did most of the chores in the home before and after school, thereby alienating them from play, schoolwork, or homework.

Chapter 14

Scars of the Trade - Servant Hood

About twelve years old, Daniel was playing hide and seek with his young masters, his master's youngest daughter and her two grandsons. Daniel was an expert at the game. His jungle instincts made him intriguing and almost invincible. He hid himself so well that his young master passed by him twice. When she was about to give up, he sprung at her from under some flower bushes. Reacting instinctively to fear, she struck at her young servant on the left front of his forehead. The enameled drinking cup gashed an area about an inch long and an inch wide on his forehead. Daniel went crying to the master who did nothing but laugh at the crying, bleeding boy. Later she placed an old rag on the wound. She told the boy to keep his hand on the rag until the wound stopped bleeding. She then put some heavy grease over it to stop the bleeding and possible infection. She simply fussed at her baby daughter, "You better not hit that boy with no cup, you hear?"

"Yes, Ma," she replied with a grin on her face. Then she remarked, 'He shouldn't have scared me!"

Of the many beatings the boy received, the worst was from J. W. Green. One day the boy was playing soccer with three grandsons of J. W. and J. W.'s own grown male servant, J. B. Daniel, skilled in soccer, was in a hurry to score on the opposing team. He tilted the ball and kicked it at mid-abdomen level. The ball hit Kylus in the stomach. The unfortunate incident happened exactly as J. W. walked outside the house. The young master screamed to the top of his lungs, holding his stomach. J. W. grabbed a steel rod, 6 inches long by 1/2" thick, from the gate to her porch and beat Daniel with it unmercifully. She beat the boy directly in the head. The boy too, screamed from the terrible blows from J. W.'s heavy hands. She was a big stocky woman.

As if waking from a daze, she asked her Young grandson if he was okay. The child replied, "Yes, grandma." Then she realized she had let rage get the best of her. She was all dressed to go out. She had gotten some of Daniel's blood on her hand. She called the boy for a closer examination of the wounds she had caused. A professional nurse, she immediately sent the servant boy to the hospital, where she was the head honcho. She gave the boy a name to ask for, "and let him take care of that wound," she told the boy. Almost immediately before the boy turned to walk away towards the hospital, she apologized to him. She said she was sorry and angry when she took the gate bar as a switch. The crying boy accepted her apology with a nod of his bleeding head.

The hospital was only about a block away from the house. J. W. had applied some tissue on the wound to stop the bleeding. She told Daniel to keep his hand on it until he reached the hospital. Upon reaching the hospital hurriedly, the boy asked for the person J. W. had told him earlier. A male doctor walked up to him and immediately cleaned the wounded area and cut the surrounding hair. He gave the boy four stitches in his head wounds without deadening the area. The boy was brave and took the stitches biting on his teeth. The nurse cleaned the boy's head and sent him back home. The boy had stopped crying by now but was still bitter inside, because he felt that the master had treated him unfairly.

He also laughed to himself when he was too angry to cry. It was a technique he had developed subconsciously to deal with whipping pain, perhaps even when his own mother whipped him.

It was late in the year 1961, Daniel was approximately thirteen years old and in the third grade. He liked his school, especially its official uniform of white pants, a blue shirt, and a red hat or baseball cap. This official uniform was worn on parade days or official days. On regular school days, uniforms were not mandatory. For one reason, most parents or guardians could not afford a uniform. Secondly, it was not yet a popular idea for public schools, but private schools wore them year round. Daniel knew because his young masters (including his master's two grandsons) wore uniforms daily to school. So did Kay-Jay.

Daniel was lucky during this year to inherit hand-me-down shoes from England. They no longer fit Moss, his friend. Moss had told him that one of the rich family's son had brought them from England, but they no longer fit the son either and they were handed down to Moss. Daniel believed the all leather shoes impressed Kay-Jay when she first saw him. Unfortunately all the other elements that could have influenced Kay-Jay to fall for him were wrong at least according to her taste and understanding. His hand-me-down shoes were often called sand crackers, because they cracked the grains of sand on the concrete or marble floors in the house wherever he walked like the sound of a crisp cereal when milk is added.

On the concrete, sidewalk, or asphalt sidewalk and streets, the shoes made noise and attracted attention. And the boy liked that. Friends asked him at school where he got the shoes. He told them someone bought them for him in England, as if to add to the little self-respect he had.

The boy observed that the children of the masters who were living and being schooled abroad treated the servants better than those who lived at home. When they came home on vacation to visit their parents the children of that rich family from whom J. W. rented and where Daniel and his master stayed, were cordial and treated the servants with respect. The young master who gave Moss the old shoes that did not fit him was a fine example. He told Daniel those were his best shoes and that they didn't fit him anymore. That made Daniel feel good about himself that a young master all the way from England considered him an equal socially that they both should wear the same shoes. Also the young masters from abroad were considerate of their servant's feelings. They asked with the phrase "please" when requesting a chore to be done such as cleaning their room or shoes, fixing their bath, cleaning, etc. J. W.'s son, Lachelle, was very good at that. He even let the boy keep his small change after a corner store purchase run. As a result, the boy loved doing chores for Lachelle. He would use that little change to buy candy and ground peas or peanuts, which was a special treat in that part of the world.

In contrast, the young masters reared at home would use some form of sarcasm, such as screaming at the boy to make haste, to a defaming name such as "Mr. Kpesi." This name made fun of his tribal origin. It meant "you Kpelle man." The adult masters themselves used profanity along with "stupid boy". These names were employed when the masters were upset or angry with the servants, but not used as frequently as the young masters.

Chapter 15

The Load that Broke the Camel's Back

Later in 1961, the boy was told to bathe the master's only granddaughter. This was the only child of her oldest daughter and her husband. It was this family that cross-eyed Pewee and loud-mouthed Wellington lived with as servants as well as others.

On this unfortunate assignment, the thirteen-year-old servant fondled this eight or nine year old girl. This happened more than once. The young master encouraged it by saying to the servant, "wash between my legs," on more than one occasion. Nobody saw these acts and he told it to nobody. It was wrong; wrong in the sense that both of them did not know what they were doing or why they were doing it. It was childish sexual curiosity.

A few weeks after these incidents, the boy was shocked. Late one night the boy was called into the master's bedroom. He went into this room on many occasions to carry water to drink, to close the window, to turn the bed down, to cut the masters corns on her feet and other services. But on this night, to his surprise, the boy was called to powder the master's back. At his age the boy had now developed initial sexual feelings. As the boy powdered his master's back, his hand began to wander to other places that were not her back. He rubbed and powdered and felt and powdered again until he heard his master sleeping or so he thought.

The boy sneaked out of the room without further exploration of the powdering body. He tried but he was not experienced enough for his little Pot-scrubbing fingers to Penetrate some sexual orifices on that body. Whether the boy's decision to quit powdering exploration of that body and leave the scene was premature is not known for sure. Should he have stayed and felt something like that of the granddaughter? The boy contemplated it long, but he was not sure what consequences might follow. After these incestful incidents, the boy continued to do his daily chores and go to his afternoon school. In approximately a month after the incidents, the boy went to school on an unforgettable Friday. It was on Fridays that the grade school children had physical education. On this unfortunate Friday, physical education lasted a little longer than usual, about half an hour more. The boys hurried home as usual to beat the sunset, just as darkness began to cover the face of the African planet. As the boys walked into the yard, they suspected nothing wrong. But on J. W.'s porch, the same porch whose gate handle had ripped Daniel's head with wounds and blood by J.W.'s heavy hands, sat Daniel's two masters. J. W. being one of them. On that same porch sat Moss's master. She was the landlord of the entire estate. She and her husband owned these properties including the one J. W. rented which is why I often refer to them as the rich family.

As the boys approached the women, Daniel spotted his 2'x 2' brown square box in which he kept his belongings. Beside the box he spotted his "can-bed", a military styled canvas bed. There was also an old brownish valise setting next to Daniel's belongings.

The three women talked and joked with each other about their love life. As the boy spoke the usual "hi Ma," a stillness erupted and one could hear a gnat buzz by. A carefully convincing plot had been hatched and blossomed while the boys were on their way from school. Daniel remembered his master fussing at him before for staying too long at school, especially on Fridays. On this unfortunate Friday, she had convinced Moss's master too, that the boys were playing around after school and were not coming straight home. J. W. suddenly screamed at him, "Take your things and go to where you've been. I'm tired of your hardheadedness." Before she could adjust her mouth from speaking, Moss's master let him have it in almost the same words. But Daniel was shocked; so he could not hear word for word what Moss's master way saying. The two were put out instantly. Daniel looked at Moss in disbelief as if to say, "where in the hell can we go?"

As Daniel kneeled to pick up his things, his master told him to leave the can bed she had bought for him. Moss picked up his old valise and tucked it under his arm. Daniel held his box in front of him with both hands. The two boys walked away slowly into the street through a parking garage where Moss's male master's car was usually parked. Daniel was not initially afraid. Moss had often talked about his uncle who had his own house near their school. Moss had also warned him that his uncle was a drunk. This uncle often worked hard for low wages as a carpenter, and he always drank away the little he earned. Moss told Daniel his uncle got drunk, made noise, and then slept off the hangover. He did not eat much either, Moss warned.

Chapter 16

The Stench Of Mud Island

"We are going to stay with my uncle," Moss told Daniel. He was already aware that Daniel did not have any relatives in Monrovia. Daniels Cousin George had gone up country to take a job at a mining company—The boys talked as they hurried through the darkened streets. There were and are still no streetlights in this African city—The boys neared the unpaved street full of shanty houses. The ghetto smell of filth and smoke filled the air and their nostrils. Mosquitoes were beginning to fly into their faces and hair and biting their arms and legs exposed by shorts, short-sleeved shirts and bare feet.

As the boys approached the zinc shack where Moss's uncle lived, the stench of the Polluted Mud swamp overpowered them. They stopped and looked at each other in awe. Then they managed to laugh out loud in disgust. This diffused their emotions fearful as they approached this dreaded shack that was to be their possible new home.

The so-called house had been built on a useless piece of discarded government swampland. Yes, the government polluted because the government did not have a sewer drainage system within this part of the city. The neighboring shanty town dwellers dumped their dirty water into this swamp after washing clothes, pots and pans, and even emptied leftover bucket bath water into the swamp.

The swamp was about the size of a city block of most urban ghettos. Dirt was dumped into it from every side. An outside bath shack and latrine were built on it also. The outside bath shack and latrine were about fifty yards away. It had only a front door, no back door and one wooden window in each of the three rooms. There was also a small entry porch. Residents had to walk on bits and pieces of planks as walkways to get into the house because of the water surrounding it. Immediately and without much thought, the boys named this new residence "Mud Island" with great laughter and the inevitable jokes. Because of the constant standing water, Mud Island was the breeding grounds for mosquitoes. The boys were pestered with the irritating noisy bugs day and night. With no screen on their window and a homemade door that only Partially closed, the boys battled the bugs constantly.

Luckily for the boys, most of these mosquitoes were young, just learning to fly, and did not carry too much blood-born sickness such as yellow fever, malaria and other communicable diseases. Had that been the case, the boys would have surely died. With no money in either of the boys' pockets, hunger struck them almost immediately. For the first two weeks, the boys struggled to find food to eat. Before going to school and after school, the boys hustled trying to find odd jobs. Finally they were told of a church that might have U.S. government surplus food.

They rushed to the church but the foodstuffs were all given out. The next day they managed to get what is commonly called burgle wheat grains in a twenty-four pound bag.

There was writing on the bag as well as the words, "donated by the United States Of America and not to be sold." But the boys were starving and ended up paying about three U.S. dollars for it. The boys did not know how to prepare this strange grain. They did not have any meats or greens to cook with this unsightly, brownish, hard and chaffy grain. They ended up boiling about four cups hulls, chaffs and all. The boys knew how to cook rice, so they cooked it like rice, only longer on the open wooden hearth. Moss's uncle had a little bottle of red palm oil in the house. The boys begged him for some and he obliged, but fussed about them finding work to do.

The next day the boys went job hunting. Daniel had never worked for pay before or even looked for work before. Besides in Monrovia, the boys did not know where to go to find a job. As fate would have it, the boy saw a sign from some sort of clothing import company. With no previous work experience, but with a praying, hopeful heart, the boy walked up two flights of stairs. He took in a deep breath and exhaled the stale, tiring, and fearful gases that tried to fill his stomach with nervous butterflies. He knocked on the door.

A young black man opened the door. He asked the boy what he wanted. The nervous boy answered, "I am looking for work." The man looked back inside the building to talk to someone, but the boy could not see. The man was still holding the door, partially opened. Inside someone gave him the okay to let the boy in. When he closed the door, the boy saw a slender, tall white male and his partner sitting at a table. They were doing some sort of paperwork.

He motioned with his hands to the boy to go sit at another table that was void of anything. He asked the boy what type of work he could do. To the boy, this question was frightening because he had never worked before. The boy explained that he had cleaned his "ex-master's house well and had washed their clothes. This was done weekly before he went to school in the afternoon," he explained to the man. The white man told him to go sit with the three black men working in a large office. They were at the other end of the room away from the two white men.

The black men asked the boy several questions, as if he were under investigation and interrogation. Then they began to tease and tell the boy that he was going to work at this man's house, that this man had a beautiful young wife, and that the boy should work well with her. They said this loud enough for the young white men to hear them. As if they were teasing him, one commented, "are you going to take this handsome sly-looking young man to your house and is

43

the missie there too?" And they all laughed at the young white men who just nodded their heads at them as if saying no in disgust. At this point, the young white man took the boy downstairs. They got into his faded yellow Volkswagen Beetle. The young boss took the boy to his house across the city to a subdivision called Point Four.

This is the same part of the city where the boy and LaFant, another servant, had lived briefly together with their masters. The young boss showed Daniel the house inside and out. He told Daniel that he would start work the next day when his wife would be home.

The boy guessed it was a safety strategy to protect their goods in their rented townhouse. After all, the boy was a stranger. in this part of the world, where there is no personal identification such as social security cards, driver's license, etc., anybody could be somebody else. The chance of finding a person, especially if he went into the interior, is very slim. However, foreign residents did hire indigenous to do housework and chores like Daniel.

Daniel believed the young boss's wife worked at the German Embassy or a school operated by foreign diplomats for their children. The man would take her to work early in the morning before the boy got there to work. They both would return at lunchtime. He would leave her home and return to his small import company office. The boy's job was basically cleaning up the house, and the pots and pans. He did not do any laundry.

One day this couple had a heated argument speaking in German and the boy could not understand what it was about. After this the boy's short assignment of three weeks ended abruptly. Daniel believes his guardian angel was close by and listening to his inner cry because after a week of eating burgle wheat, the boy ran into an old acquaintance. This fellow, Harold, had known Daniel and also knew Daniel's master who had put him out. He told Daniel that he just happened to be in the neighborhood, stopped by Daniel's old residence, and had found out that Daniel had been put out. The reason was not given to him. Harold knew that Daniel was a good servant. He tried to convince Daniel that it was just a misunderstanding and that he could take Daniel back to his original master and convince her to take Daniel back. But the boy was a strong-willed child. He felt he had done nothing to deserve being put out at night. Daniel refused to go back to his old master. Harold tried several times to convince the boy but to no avail.

He finally told the boy of another lady he knew well. In fact, Harold told the boy that this new "master-to-be" was from his tribal county and they spoke the same dialect, mano. The lady had several children. Another factor that helped Daniel decide about this new lady master, was the fact that her house was right across from Daniel's schoolhouse. Daniel agreed for Harold to talk to this woman. The next day, Harold came and got Daniel and his belongings box and took him to this new master.

Chapter 17

Second Master - More a Mother than a Master

Daniel was more than surprised when he arrived to meet his new master. The new master greeted him with open arms, sort of a hug, but not close to her body. She told Harold that the boy spoke good English. She told Harold and Daniel that her two youngest children, a boy eight years old and his sister six years old, were gone to school. Daniel would stay and help take care of them whenever she went out.

Harold and the new master had a lengthy talk in their native Mano dialect so the boy could not understand what they talked about. But he believed it was a sort of what do you know of him conversation. After they finished, the new master asked Daniel if he was hungry. Daniel responded, "yes," with his head rather than his voice, which was barely audible.

The master gave him a piece of bread and a cup of cold water. The boy surveyed the house with his eyes. He found that there was a small shop in the front room. It was not much of a shop; there was not much on the shelves except a few cans and a jar of chicken bouillon cubes, actually known as magic cubes. It was sold per cube for five cents each. The boy did know prices for the other items yet.

This was a late Friday afternoon. Soon the children arrived home from a neighboring school. They greeted Daniel with a smiling "hi" and a shaking of hands. The boy child told Daniel of his other brothers and an older sister, who were in a mission school, out of the capital city and the county, a driving distance of approximately two and a half hours away..

At evening time they all sat in the small front shop-like room and talked. Mostly Daniel was told that his biggest and most important responsibility would begin the next Monday, a school day. He was to walk the little girl to her school, which was two blocks away from the house. Since the little girl's school was a Catholic all-girls school, the eight-year-old brother went to a different school. It also was in walking distance from their house. He usually walked with other neighbor kids to and from school each day.

Late that evening the boy met Edo, an older male servant. Since he had joined the Army, the master understood and let him go to training and camp every so often. Edo's main chore was to wash the clothes. He usually did this on the weekend. But this came to a halt, after he found out that Daniel could wash clothes as well. Edo began to stay at camp late on the weekends. Soon the boy was told to handle the washing.

Soon after this, Edo started having problems obeying the master. He felt he was too big to be told what to do. He moved out on his own near the Army barracks. After this Edo came by from time to time to see how things were at the house. He finally stopped coming to the house although the boy saw him in various parts of the city on occasion.

The following year in 1962 the boy was promoted to the fourth grade, which he completed. The boy began his fifth grade class in a new public school in 1963. The school was called the Monrovia Demonstration Elementary School. It was the same school his previous master's youngest daughter and two grandsons attended. And it was the same school Kay-Jay had attended. But it was now somewhat run down and converted to a public school after the private school vacated. He was now settled with his new master, who treated him with respect and some dignity. For one thing, the boy did not get whipped anymore. Yes he still did chores that the new master's children did not do, but he was talked to decently and there was no name-calling, putting down and no teasing yet. The boy now began to enjoy some extracurricular activities like soccer, ping-pong and more other than regular school work. He became active in the local YMCA. At the YMCA he was involved in Christian social clubs and sports activities.

The boy survived the fifth grade and began to build reputation as a good speller. in the sixth grade, he represented his class at a spelling bee contest and won. He played soccer for his class and his school although he was an average player. He also became an amateur photographer, a hobby he kept up for a while. Although he and his friend Moss no longer lived together or attended the same school, they managed to keep in contact.

At the end of the sixth grade year in 1964 his master told him that he was growing up and that he needed to find a little job to help himself and to support all of his activities and hobbies. The reason given was that his master had four other children, all in a private mission school. She told the boy she was unable to care for her children's needs and be able to help the boy with all of his needs.

The following week, Daniel began looking for a part time job. He needed something he could do and still go to school. He remembered his sixth grade Peace Corps teachers, especially Mrs. Grahl and her husband. They had mentioned the Peace Corps office being midtown, near the market place. Daniel thought, why not try this. He may as well go there and check for a cleaning boy job or an errand boy job. Luckily for Daniel he met the Prunty's. This New Jersey couple was very nice. They interviewed Daniel and told him he could start the next week. The job paid twelve dollars a month to start and Daniel had to work only twice a week. It later paid fifteen dollars a month with him working three days per week. He worked as a house boy for a Peace Corps volunteer family, enabling him to support his needs.

The boy now had to register at a private Wilson Afternoon School. His reason was twofold; first his previous school ended at the sixth grade level and the only public junior and senior high school was to far to leave work Friday evenings and get there on time. At this new school, the boy made lots of new friends. He also made decent grades. The boy also started shyly liking girls. From time to time he would be asked for some of the little money he made. He would give what he had left to his master or he now refers to her as a stepmother.

While he was in the seventh grade, Daniel's master had built another house that was on a plot of land that she had bought a long time ago. The contractor finished the walls of the foundation and the boy was instructed to go each day and fill in the hollowed foundation with sand. He had to do this chore with a shovel and a bucket. There was no wheel barrel available. As the truck dumped the pile of sand near the high walls, the boy would fill the bucket put it on his head, walk up on a wooden makeshift stairs, and dump the sand in the foundation. There was this concession to the contractor so that his fees would be lowered. It took the boy about a month to complete filling the foundation. Afterwards six-rooms zinc flat was built on top of the foundation. Even at this stage and age, the boy slept on a makeshift bed or a mat on the floor of the master's boy's room.

After filling foundation of the house where the boy did not have a room, but slept on the floor, he was given additional task of digging a six-by-six foot hole for the family "w.c." The "w.c." short for water closet is a common name for the outside latrine. The boy began this arduous task in the late evenings after school. In the morning he had household chores. Hence he could not do the digging at that time. He attended private school in the afternoon between 1:00 and 5:00 p.m. As he dug deeper and deeper into this hard rock he began to notice some form of deposits on some of the hard flat rocks. Those rocks were usually crusted together. The deposits were in between them. The boys rudimentary education led him to believe that those deposits were some kind of oil. Exactly what kind of oil he could not tell. He did not have the proper level of education nor the necessary tools to analyze the foreign deposits on the rocks. Though he got help from other boys in the neighborhood and a little hired hand he paid with giving food, the boy eventually finished digging the hole for the water closet. A hired carpenter eventually built a makeshift shack over the hole for privacy. It was built with some zinc sheet metal and had a small door.

In 1966 as the boy entered the eighth grade, his master's four other children from the mission school returned home. She now had enough room to accommodate them. She said that she could no longer afford to keep them in the mission school. Besides, the two oldest children had completed their high school and she did not want the other two younger ones to remain without older sibling protection.

When the other children arrived, the youngest boy who had lived at home all along snitched on the boy Daniel. Before moving into this new zinc house, Daniel and other neighbor kids had crashed a rich man's party not far from their

47

old house. Daniel had drunk a little too much. He began to demand the rich man's servant daughter named Trerese to come outside because he was in love with her. Daniel had never said anything to this girl about being in love with her until that day. The liquor had simply brought out his inner desire for this girl. Even if the girl had noticed him before and had any desire to be his girl, he had just ruined such a chance. He had made a fool of himself. The girl's father made the other children at the party take Daniel home and put him to bed.

The next day Daniel heard the story of how he got drunk and began to demand that Trerese come outside, so that he could see and talk to her. The unfortunate incident became a neighborhood joke on Daniel for a long time. But he lived through it and one day he saw Trerese and apologized for the mess he had made that night. She gave him a beautiful smile and remarked "it's okay."

As the boy reflected back on his life at that time, he remembered that he had gotten drunk two other times and after waking up the next day was shameful for his acts. The Trerese incident was the third shameful public display of his young life. From that day forward, Daniel vowed never to get drunk on any occasion again. Reflecting on his partying and young drinking Life, he remembers his friends and the general gatherings of which he wrote this poem:

In the Pursuit of Pleasure

The super genius mix with the sensible
And the genius with the fool
To accomplish a single aim
To seek fun and pleasures
Not happiness
For happiness is attained
As a victory over problems
A wise man may indulge
In the foolishness of a fool
Not to become foolish
But to whet wisdom into him (foolish man)

- JD -

Daniel was now a teenager in the ninth grade. He found new employment at the only intercontinental hotel in the country, which was in Monrovia. A member of the janitorial crew, he worked days and attended evening school. The only public senior high school in the suburb of Monrovia was called Tubman High School named after the then president of Liberia. The boy remained at this school and completed the ninth and tenth grades. These were some of the best times he ever had. With two friends named Isa and Robie, he had lots of fun in high school. Recently he learned that Isa works for the Liberian transitional (wartime) government and that Robie went overseas into the missionary field.

Daniel and the master's children grew up together as brothers and sisters. They even wore one another's clothes. They dated some of the not-so popular girls within the neighborhood. By this time the boy had had a shanty room built with used zinc on the side of the all-zinc house built by his master. The boy's shack became so popular that one of the president's sons was caught in the boy's bed. He was caught in an uncompromising position with his date. He had been brought and let in by one of Daniel's foster brothers. Daniel's master had four sons and three of them hung with Daniel to do the things that teenagers do from time to time.

They even coined a nickname "pic" denoting certain females they liked. Though not a negative name, they still called each other "pic" instead of the individual's name whenever any of the boys met or greeted each other.

Even some of their neighborhood and school associates stuck on the "pic" nickname and use it among themselves today. Because most of the boys from that small neighborhood moved away to different parts of the world, Daniel believes there are "pic" everywhere they go.

Daniel entered the eleventh grade and the hotel began to downsize its employee crew. He was laid off but was propositioned to be rehired, as all he had to do was sign a contract. One of the personnel managers, a homosexual told the boy he would be rehired if he would complete and sign the contract but first needed a favor. He told Daniel to come by his house. When Daniel went by this man's house, he approached him to have sex. If he would agree to have sex with him, he would rehire him in the dietary or room service department of the hotel. Daniel refused. Two weeks later, he found another job with a German company. Because the boy had a knack for photography, he was promised work in a photo lab but to the boy's surprise it was just another housekeeping job. Each time he asked his boss when he could begin his lab training, the boss said, "wait."

Being in the eleventh grade at the age of twenty-one, he had already gone through three failed love affairs but now felt strong enough for the game of love. Instead of falling in love he simply dated. Even while he was in the tenth grade, a girl said he had fathered her son. He was not certain but accepted the responsibility anyway. The child lived with him.

Daniel soon found out that his German boss was also interested in him as more than just a housecleaning employee. He started making passes and gestures at Daniel. He learned the nature of his intent when he took Daniel home one evening. He told Daniel that he would teach him how to drive his white Mercedes if he became his special friend. Daniel became furious and told the white man, "I am not a homosexual, and I have a son who calls me daddy." The boss apologized saying "I'm very sorry, as I did not mean any harm. Forget the whole conversation."

49

From that point on Daniel was transferred to the laundry unit of this compound of German foreign workers. Daniel hand-washed for about four families on a weekly basis; single people, one couple, and couple with a small son. The boy kept his job hoping to be transferred to the photo lab, but his hope never materialized.

He finally graduated from the twelfth grade in 1970. He never felt prouder of himself than when the secretary of state for Liberia presented him his diploma. The boy was an excellent student. He was class president in the tenth grade and class vice president in the eleventh grade. He represented his school at the Model UN General Assembly at city hall after a conference of high school seniors in Harper, Cape Palmas, Liberia among other accomplishments.

The boy graduated from the Student Union Institute, a night high school. He attended night school because he had to work, and also take care of a son as a single parent.

The baby's mother relinquished all her responsibility and rights to him when the baby was just six months old. The mother simply said that the baby was hindering her from doing her personal things and that Daniel should take his son and raise him. He took his son and with help from relatives up country and his foster brothers and sisters, he did manage to care for and raise his baby son.

By this time Daniel's job with the German company had ended. The people for whom he washed had completed their assignment in Liberia and had left. This included the German fellow who wanted to have homosexual relations with him. After Daniel's refusal, the older fellow imported one of his former lovers from the African country of Dahomey. The young black fellow though with light complexion had told Daniel that the German man was his uncle. But the boy knew better. He was this German man's lover. He later told Daniel he had lived with this German fellow before in Norway.

Daniel's graduation freed him to try to find a better job. After all he had not only himself to support, he now had a three-year old son to care for. He was also expected to help his tribal parents and siblings, as this is a cultural tradition. Daniel's foster stepmother sent him to a man she knew at the Liberian Refinery Company. Daniel waited all morning to talk to him. After the man had returned from lunch, he spoke with Daniel, but did not like what the man had to say. The oil refinery was not hiring at the time. Daniel went home very disappointed and told his foster stepmother what the man said.

After meeting up with one of his closest friends in high school, Robie, it appears Robie knew a man in the refinery's personnel office named Mitch. This man really liked and respected Robie. Robie gave Daniel a note to take to Mitch who told Daniel to come back the next day. Mitch sent Daniel to be processed for employment. Daniel was hired in the laboratory as a petroleum sample collector. The job was very dangerous but Daniel who had very little training, learned the hard way. He discovered dangers in the tank fields daily as he worked. The refinery was built in an isolated wooded and grassy part of the suburbs of Monrovia. Snakes, an explosion of a tank, and the eminent danger of slipping and falling were always present in Daniel's mind. And once he slipped but managed to grab a rail on this hot fuel oil tank. The incident scared Daniel terribly, almost forcing him to quit this job. But he had a goal in mind and stayed on the job for over 2 years.

At the beginning of this refinery job, the boy's foster stepmother had asked him to move out on his own since he now had a regular job. Daniel complied, though he was not sure where to go. He had never lived alone before. Daniel managed to find a room near the refinery and later moved and lived with one of the daughters of his landlord.

Daniel had a very close friend in the United States who was also a distant cousin. He was determined to go to the United States for college. He therefore tried saving a little whenever he could. His girlfriend's house was full of people and he and his girl had often to feed some of the children, sisters, and their mothers in the house. He also ended up fathering another son by this girl.

While working in the laboratory of L. R. C., he befriended two young men. They ended up calling each other cousins. Their friendship grew so strong that others working in the same lab began hating them. The three guys even dreamed up the silly idea that one day when they became wealthy, they would build a villa and call it Villa Couse. It was to mean villa of cousins. Daniel believes the other two members of the dreaming trio have lost hope. Marauding civil wars have taken a very heavy toll on their lives only sparing their souls. But one day Daniel believes that Villa Couse could become a reality.

The boy was promoted to laboratory tester after two years and four months on the job. He also received a certificate for training as a fire fighter in January of 1974. By this time the boy's plan of going to the United States was coming together slowly. He now communicated more often with dear friend cousin in the United States. Daniel visited the U.S. embassy in Monrovia to inquire as to what he would need to travel to the United States for college. He had already acquired his immigration papers and forms from the U.S. school that accepted him. This form is the formal acceptance for a foreign student to attend a U.S. college.

Chapter 18

Snakes in the Way

After the boy had all the necessary papers required by the U.S. Embassy for travel, he ran into a snag. People who had traveled to the United States for school told him that he did not have to have lots of money in his pocket to travel. He found out almost too late that he must have eight hundred dollars as traveling money before he would be allowed into the United States. This was just for pocket change, in case an emergency occurred.

The boy had already borrowed five hundred dollars from a local bank to help him purchase his ticket. He had only about three hundred dollars left for pocket change. This eight hundred-dollar requirement caused the boy to have sleepless nights. He had no one to turn to for the money. He managed to convince his landlord/mother-in-law to help. She in turn gave Daniel the deed to the land and house they were living in. Daniel was to try his best to pawn this deed to someone trustworthy and borrow five hundred dollars. The boy went everywhere including one of the president's sons to pawn this deed, but no one would help. The boy was distressed. In the end, the boy turned to God and began to pray. He knew that if any one could help him with this problem, it would be his creator and savior. The boy was so distressed about not having the eight hundred dollars that he missed his original flight. Daniel left both his sons with his fiancée and her parents who owned the building the two of them were previously renting.

On the following Wednesday the boy boarded a Pan Am 747 for the United States. This was June 1974, a day he'll never forget. Even the President's son to whom the boy tried to pawn his landlord's deed commented that the boy was lucky to have been granted a visa for school during the early summer. It was his experience that the U.S. Immigration Service frowned on foreign students being in the United States at such time when most schools were out.

The boy's flight seemed eternal, with one stop over in another African country called Dakar. The flight lasted about eleven hours and forty-five minutes. Maybe it was just the time zone that made the boy's flight seem everlasting. Perhaps it was the fear of not having the eight hundred dollars. But most assuredly, the fear of being sent back home because of not having the required money put a butterfly in the boy's stomach until he arrived in New York's J.F.K. Airport.

The boy's prayer was so intense that you probably could see piety on his lips, face, and chest where his heart is located, especially when he watched the immigration officer in charge of letting people in to the United States. The officer was tough and mean. As the boy became the number two man in line to

53

face this immigration monster, an important phone call came in for him. "Praise the Lord," the boy whispered inwardly so loud that it came out, rollng on his lips and face. An older black officer took charge. He processed the next person in front of the boy fast. He took the boy's passport, then asked for the rest of his papers. Daniel gave him everything. He was still praying that the man did not ask to see his pocket change money. And thank heavens he did not! He let the boy through the gate and said, "Welcome to the United States." The boy smiled and answered back with a handshake. Free at last, free at last, thank God, Daniel was free at last!

The boy was now relieved of this heart-stopping and head-aching pocket change problem, at least for the moment. He quickly dodged the cabby, who tried to grab his luggage. He thought the boy was going somewhere in the Big Apple. Instead the boy rushed to the airport shuttle bus that had just pulled up. He was in a hurry to catch a connecting flight from New York's LaGuardia Airport to Cleveland's Hospkins Airport. Luckily for the boy the connecting flight from LaGuardia was delayed.

He booked his reservation and sat down. He dozed until someone reminded him that Cleveland flight was ready for boarding. He got a wing seat, and began to watch parts of the Big Apple for real, apart from book and magazine pictures he had seen before. His second flight ever landed safely in Cleveland late in the evening. Leaving Cleveland, he hurriedly boarded another bus and asked to be dropped off at the nearest Greyhound Bus Station. From there, the boy would take his last ride for his final destination—Toledo, Ohio.

While he waited to board the bus, he spotted a small bar just near the comer of the bus station. He quickly asked when the bus would depart. He checked his little brown face watch and reasoned that he had enough time to buy and drink his first American beer. When he asked the bartender for beer, the question to him was, "which one?" Since the boy did not know that America had so many varieties of beer, he replied "the cheapest one." The bartender looked at him and smiled as he collected the dollar out of the boy's hand. "You must be new here," he commented. "Yes," the boy replied. "I can tell from the way you are dressed," the man asserted.

Daniel was wearing what was commonly referred to as the total involvement suit—casual short-sleeved jacket, shirt, and matching pants. It had four pockets—two medium on the breast areas and two larger ones on each side of the abdomen. This semi casual suit was so named after the nineteenth president of Liberia, William R. Tolbert, was sworn into office wearing a white version of the suit. Since Tolbert's first political slogan was "total involvement," the suit became commonly known as the "total involvement suit". The bartender served the boy Stroh's beer in a bottle, and it tasted great. In Liberia there is only one local brew called Club beer. The imported beers at the time were Heineken beer and Guinness Stout beer.

After about two hours on the bus the boy finally reached his cousin in Toledo, Ohio. Three weeks in America Daniel got a letter from one of his closest friends and coworkers back in Liberia. To his astonishment, the boy learned that one of his former supervisors had gone to the Liberia Refinery Company's management and advised them that the boy had not completed paying off his little loan. He was paying this loan off through a payroll deduction. He requested that management call the United States Immigration, so that they would stop the boy at J.F.K from entering the United States. To him the boy had committed the ultimate crime of failure to pay off his entire loan before going away. The move by the boy, he told management, might prevent the bank from giving loans to other employees.

According to this friend the management replied on the contrary, that this young man went to improve himself educationally. "In fact," the manager said, "when he returns and more like him, we can stop importing the expensive foreign employees who make more money than us. Besides salary they get company cars, housing allowances, etc." In fact, according to Daniel's friend, management even laughed at such a ridiculous idea as deporting a young aspiring citizen of his own country. Daniel did pay off his loan in about a year after his arrival in the United States.

Chapter 19

Jimi and the American Experience

The boy, now going by the name "Jimi", was not too surprised by the American country and its people. He had had a few American friends, teachers, and employers, and had seen a lot of America on TV, in books, and in the verbal and written media. He entered the U.S. in June and began school in September of 1974. He quickly made friends with both sexes. In fact he felt that the American girls were friendlier than the guys.

In school, some of his African-American friends felt he was too friendly with everybody referring to both whites and blacks. Jimi let those people know that where he came from there was no prejudice between whites and blacks. Between the two classes of blacks (the haves and the have-nots), one could feel some sense of jealousy, but not open hatred as in America between whites and blacks.

After one quarter in his first school Jimi realized that he did not like this school and the curriculum in which he was enrolled. He changed to a new school further away from the city. This meant that he had now incurred additional expenses. He must now find a part time job to help himself with additional school expenses. He had to find a part-time job.

He found a job at a gas station. He would come from school, change clothes, and go straight to work. He worked from about 3 p.m. to closing at 7 p.m. He made minimum wage at the gas station, but a few good citizens tipped him. He rode a special bus to his school sometimes; other times, he rode with friends. He also rode the city transit bus to his part-time job and whenever he was going downtown.

During the boy's first winter snowstorm, he was appalled. He marveled how water vapor is made into fine ice in the sky and falls back down to the ground. He played in the snow. He even threw snowballs with a stranger at the bus stop. The bus was so slow coming that day, so he began to walk to work. It was about an hour's walk, but snow was falling on his face and head. The boy did not mind the sweat under his blue jean jacket because it was well insulated. He got to work about 4 p.m. and closed early about 6 p.m. due to the heavy snowfall. The boy survived his first winter in America. During the following year, the company changed management and relocated the gas station at which the boy worked.

Chapter 20

The Eagle Swooped

The boy continued to work part-time and go to college. It was early spring, and the air was brisk one bright sunny evening. He had just come from school. He had taken off his shirt, put food on the stove and began cooking his dinner. Suddenly there was a knock on his door. Thinking that it might be one of his neighbors or friends, he went with no shirt on and opened the door. The two men at the door represented the eagle, —the United States Immigration Services! The boy was shocked that the I.N.S. would come to his house. The two men identified themselves and asked to come in. The boy obliged and let them in. They began to ask questions - if the boy was in school and how many hours was he taking per quarter. Luckily the boy had a copy of his college schedule lying on the living room table beside his textbooks. After the boy had answered their questions, they looked at each other.

One asked if the boy was working. As if to entrap the boy, he looked hard at the boy. The boy quickly answered yes, but qualified his answer with, "only part-time at the gas station." At that point the second agent asked why only part time. Jimi said because he needed additional money for his new school. He had changed his field of study and his new major had several small labs involved in the course.

He also had to travel further for school compared to the first school, which was downtown on a bus route. He also told the agent that the reason he needed to work part-time was that his uncle who was helping him to pay his school fees had died of heart problems.

It was the same nonexistent uncle whose name Jimi had used to prepare his affidavit of support while he studied in the United States. This lie was just the tip of the iceberg. People do all kinds of untruthful things every day just to enter the United States.   This is especially common among citizens of third world countries. So it was in the beginning of the boy's plan to enter the United States that he told his first white lie to get the necessary requirements for the I.N.S.

Therefore, the story of the death of his uncle was the finishing touch on his original white lie, which was on his affidavit of support for admission into the United States. But regardless of Jimi's story, he had faith in his plan, in himself, and in his ambition to work very hard to make his plan a reality.

The boy inquired whether the school had reported him for a reason. The agents replied "no, it was not the school, but someone had reported him and others that they were not in school, so we're supposed to check such leads," they said. The two agents left and Jimi sighed with relief. The boy suspected he knew the snake that had ratted on him to the Immigration Service, but he thought to himself, "That snake will have his day."

Chapter 21

The American Experience Continues

The relocation of the gas station for which the boy worked posed another hardship for him. It was in an area that did not have a full bus service. The bus stopped and turned around more than two miles away from this new location. When the bus dropped the boy off and turned to go back downtown, he had to walk the rest of the way to work. Sometimes he got lucky and hitched a ride to work. Most days he walked and reached work tired and sweaty.

Soon during this time, a young neighbor of the gas station began to visit the service station constantly. He would bring his bike to work on, borrowing tools from the boy. One day he struck up a conversation about his friend who had an old car for sale. Even though the boy did not have a driver's license yet, he told the gas station neighbor to let his friend bring the car so he could check it out. Soon he did and a deal was struck. The boy spent about two hundred and fifty dollars on this old Ford. Although the boy had not driven officially, he began to teach himself on the grounds of the service station. He would leave the car there after work and walk until he gets a ride or walks to a bus zone. In about three days the boy went to sign up to get his driver's license. In three weeks Jimi was a licensed driver and a car owner.

Since he taught himself to drive, he had not learned to change lanes properly. On his way to school driving himself for the first time on a public street and highway, an old man rear-ended him. Since he was a new driver and spoke with a foreign accent, the police ticketed him. The boy was cited for improper lane change. He did not know about auto liability insurance and he did not have any. The officer however, did not fine the student on his way to school, but told him and the accident victim to work out the insurance settlement. After school, the boy went to the old man's insurance company. He signed restitution papers for the $1200 in damages he had supposedly caused. Jimi kept his job at the gas station until the following incident occurred.

Station Attendant Fights, Foils Armed Robbery Try

Handgun Dropped Twice In Struggle

A daring act of wrestling with two would-be robbers, one of them armed with a gun, averted a loss Friday night at the Gasown service station, 1610 North Reynolds Rd.

Two men entered the station shortly before 10 p.m. and began talking with attendant Jim Dillon. One of them drew a handgun, police said.

Mr. Dillon immediately pushed the man closest to him into the man with the gun, knocking him into a glass door, which broke, causing him to drop the gun, police said. The man regained possession of the gun, while Mr. Dillon and the other man struggled. But the attendant pushed one man into the other again, and again the gun was knocked to the floor.

When the man recovered the weapon this time, he yelled to the other and both fled on foot, having taken no money, police were told.

A customer on a motorcycle said he followed the suspects for a short way but was ordered at gunpoint to turn back.

Mr. Dillon was not injured.

The only clues left for police were several pink hair curlers which fell from one of the suspects during the struggle.

After the attempted robbery, Jimi realized that he had fractured his left thumb. A doctor treated his thumb with a cast at a local hospital. While he was off work, still shaken from the incident, his supervisor called not to thank him, not to see how he was doing, but to chew him out.

The supervisor's concern was that in a situation like that the boy should let the robbers take the money. After all, the service station had insurance, he said. But in such split-second decision making, Jimi was only concerned about saving his life. After all, the boy had heard over the news, right before he was attacked that in the past three weeks, one of the same company's gas stations he worked at had been robbed and the attendant killed. The boy was taking no chances. That was the frame of his mind when he fought off his attackers. And thank God he did, perhaps he prolonged his life. The boy was replaced while he was still on sick leave. He was never fired officially from the job.

After this unfortunate incident, Jimi healed in about six weeks. He managed to find employment at a local auto spring manufacturing plant. The wages here were better than the gas station job and far more lucrative than his petrochemical laboratory-testing job in his former country.

In this factory he worked the second shift. He found out that several of his countrymen worked in this factory on the morning shift. Most of these men had recently moved to Toledo from Philadelphia. "The eagle swooped down again catching several prey all at once this time."

On the job just about three months, the boy learned that immigration officers had raided the small factory and seized a few illegal aliens who worked there. Thank God the boy was not one of them, at least not yet. He learned that most of the guys who moved into Toledo, Ohio from Philadelphia, Pennsylvania were illegal or had failed to go to school as they had claimed to do when they came into the United States. This put the boy on edge. He also learned that one of the captives had squealed on other Liberians working at this factory. This "sell out" of his countrymen was in a deal made for leniency in their charges and treatment. The eagle stalked other preys in approximately six weeks. Jimi and another Liberian student working the night shift. They were also not at peace since this unfortunate incident. But since no man knew the hour when the sons of the eagle would swoop down again, they kept on working and tried not to worry about it. One night there was a quiet wagging of the supervisor's hand and their names were called in a low tone. "Come here quick," he demanded.

Jimi and Andy ran to the supervisor. He yelled, "go, back door, over the fence, now! Immigration officers are coming to find more of you!"

Jimi had papers as a student only, but not for working in the United States. Like sprinting and long jump gladiators, Jimi and Andy scaled the high barbed-wire fence like it was not even there. They crossed a railroad track and ran into the brush of a neighbor's yard, hoping some dog did not attack them or give them away as escapees. The immigration officers did search the factory despite the supervisor's advice that the boys had gone home earlier. They told the supervisor that they had information that other illegal aliens especially from Liberia and Nigeria were employed in that factory besides those captured in their earlier raid.

All the Liberian workers were hard workers, and the supervisors liked that. They would put out the required production quota in one half to three fourths of the allowed time. The supervisor would make them clean up the factory and let them sit out the rest of the time. Some even left early and the supervisor would cover for them. He said as long as production quotas were met, he did not care what the boy and others did with the rest of their time.

The supervisor, Duell, called the boy and Andy at home. He told them, "Do not come back to work until you have proper papers to work." The supervisor had to cover himself as well as protect his job, he told the boys. Jimi was dating an American girl and he told her what had happened. They had already made plans to marry in December of 1976 on his birthday. The wedding was quickly rescheduled for early summer of that year. Once the boy got married, he could go back to work without fear of being arrested by Immigration. He and his wife went downtown, filed the necessary papers, and the boy returned to work in August of 1976.

He stayed in that job and stayed in school, from which he graduated in June 1977. The factory in which he worked so hard closed in December 1979 due to cheaper labor in Canada where it relocated. Following is a letter (exhibit A) that broke Jimi's heart and crushed many other family men, which thought that by working very hard, they had a secure future.

Andy, the boy's partner in the high fence jumping crime, did not return to work. Andy was in love with a Liberian girl, and they already had a boy child. He could not do the same thing that Jimi did - marry an American girl! Andy relocated to another city and state and hoped that Andy found another way to get his Alien registration and eventually his citizenship. The boy named his first American son after his old friend, Andy.

After this company closed its doors, the boy began to look for another employment. He also returned to college but with a wife, who already had two children and was not working, he quit school and got odd jobs: washing dishes in a restaurant and being a security guard. He received two commendations for a job well done as a security guard, but no raise followed, as he had been promised (see exhibit B).

He soon found another position in his area of interest. Jimi had an associate degree in law enforcement. He was hired as a private police officer for a local city mental institution. In this career-oriented job, Jimi felt he was now beginning to climb the career ladder. But twelve days before his ninety-day probation was up, he was terminated. He was told that he had missed a day not coming to work when he was called in on his day off. He was told that it was in the policy manual that if and when he was needed in emergency situations, he was to come in to work. But Jimi did not remember being called in.

He was also investigated because he had transported a wounded female mental patient to a nearby hospital. On the way to the hospital the patient had asked him for some of the lunch he was eating. He had given this mental patient a sandwich and dropped her off at the nearby hospital's emergency room. The hospital was to call the facility where the patient resided after the ER treatment, so she could be picked up.

The boy felt he was wrongly dismissed and went to the local Equal Employment Opportunity Commission (EEOC) office. He lodged a complaint about lack of evidence for dismissal. The only other African-American in the department, who was Jimi's afternoon shift supervisor, felt also that Jimi had been wrongfully dismissed. For one thing, he had never reprimanded him for doing anything wrong on his shift. He offered to testify at a hearing if one came up. He gave Jimi confidence to go ahead and file his case.

The case did not go to trial for two years. During that time, the African-American supervisor had been "bought out" by the establishment he worked for. This was only a suspicion that Jimi assumed. In this two year span, Jimi's supervisor had been promoted three times. He was a sergeant while he was the boy's supervisor, and hated the then director. He was promoted to Lieutenant, then to Captain, and eventually to Acting Director.

When the time came for the deposition in the case to determine if there was enough evidence for a trial, the sergeant - supervisor, now acting director, recanted his statement. He even denied a note he had previously signed from the boy's attorney. He stated that though he had not reprimanded the boy on his shift, he could not speak for the then director, who felt Jimi was not qualified to remain employed. Due to his refusal to testify on the boy's behalf and due to lack of evidence on both sides, the case was annulled. This was a great blow to Jimi, who had tried so desperately to stay on his career path.

The boy worked from late 1982 to early 1983 for the same security company that gave him two commendations for a job well done but would not give him a raise. Although he was being promised but those promises never materialized. He had also taken the civil service exams for the city's fire department and the city police department.

In late 1983, he received one of the finest letters he would ever get in his lifetime (see exhibits C & D). The letter informed him that he had been accepted into the city's police department. His scores from the civil service exam for both the fire and police exams were impressive. The boy quit his security job to begin his police academy training. The training began in September 1983 and ended with graduation in January 1984.

The July 1983 before the boy was accepted into the Police Academy, he had been approved to receive $87 worth of food stamps per month. The food stamp office made this determination based on Jimi's income. He had applied for help because he had two sons to support besides paying child support for a younger child with his first wife.

When the academy started in September 1983, the boy had already used the September food stamps. When the October food stamps came, the boy naturally used them to buy food for his household. He had already received a letter from his caseworker that his food stamp certification would expire by the end of October 1983. If he needed to continue to be helped, he would have to reapply.

But the boy had found a job he loved and he would not need to reapply for federal food stamps. The academy training was going well, so well that the boy and another female cadet turned down the fire department offer to make them firefighters.

Jimi Daniel Dillon

CITY OF **TOLEDO** OHIO

DIVISION OF POLICE

DAVID A. BOSTON
City Manager

C. E. Riser
Safety Director
Commissioner - Traffic Engineering

SAFETY BUILDING
525 No. Erie Street

JOHN MASON
Chief of Police
LEADS OH0480700

August 26, 1983

JIMI DILLON
132 PAGE
TOLEDO, OH 43620

Mr. Dillon,

It is my pleasure to inform you that you are a successful candidate for the position of Police Officer Trainee in the Toledo Police Division. Training will begin on Friday, September 9, 1983.

Upon your appointment as a police officer trainee on September 9, 1983, you must be a resident of the City of Toledo. Enclosed is a certification of residency form that must be signed and returned on the above date.

Upon receipt of this letter please report to the gun control office to have your City of Toledo Identification Card made prior to September 9, 1983. The gun control office is located in Suite 2000 on the 20th floor, One Government Center on the corner of Jackson and Erie St. This office is open from 8:00 a.m. until 4:30 p.m. Parking space will be available in the municipal parking lot on Orange St. between Spielbusch Ave. and Erie St.

You are to report for duty, dressed in business attire, to Captain Philip J. Moore, at 7:30 a.m., September 9, 1983, in the gymnasium of Holy Spirit Seminary at 5201 Airport Highway, on the corner of Airport Highway and Reynolds Rd. in Toledo. You can plan to spend the entire day in class with dismissal sometime after 4:30 p.m. Also, be prepared to furnish the Police Division with all the following information that is applicable.

1. Your name, social security number and date of birth.
2. Your spouse's name, social security number and date of birth.
3. Your children's names, social security numbers and dates of birth.
4. Your mother and fathers names and dates of birth.
5. The make and license number of any vehicle that you plan to drive to work.

If you have any questions, please call Sergeant Wayne Markland at 385-5701 or Sergeant George Gerken at 385-9534.

Sincerely,

John Mason
Chief of Police

Exhibit C

102

Enclosure

Criminal Justice
Coordinating Council

301 Collingwood Blvd.
Toledo, Ohio 43602

CJCC MEMBERS

Chairman:
James M. Holzemer

Vice Chairman:
Francine Lawrence

Secretary:
Charles Doneghy

Tom Bodi
Andy Devine
Joseph A. Flores
Philip A. Hawkey
Harry Kessler
Donna Owens
Anthony Pizza
James Telb
Richard Webb

CJCC PROJECTS

**Criminal Justice Training
and Education Center**
244-4680

**Northwest Ohio Regional
Information System**
244-0763

Regional Planning Unit
244-5819

According to Criminal Justice Training Center records, Jimi Dillon attended Basic Police School #82-046.

Mr. Dillon did not complete the program.

The following scores are recorded:

Laws of Arrest	82%
Search & Seizure	84%
Firearms *Attached form has range scores.	90% written exam
Emergency Vehicle Op.	80%
Ohio Court Structure	76%

Exhibit D

Jimi Daniel Dillon

NAME __Jimi Dillon__   DATE_____

	POSSIBLE	SCORE	%
LOW POINT 9' 15 SECONDS	6	6	100
TWO HAND HIGH PT. 21' 2.5 SECONDS	6	4 1 miss	66.6
MULTIPLE TARGETS 21' 4 SECONDS	12	10 1 miss	83.3
USE OF COVER 75' 45 SECONDS WEAK AND STRONG	12	–12 8 miss	00.0
LOW LEVEL LIGHT 21' 3 SECONDS	6	6	100
ZERO LIGHT 21' 3 SECONDS	6	6	100
			Avg. 74.9%

EACH HIT SCORES 1 POINT
EACH MISS DEDUCTS 2 POINTS
ROUND NOT FIRED DEDUCTS 1 POINT

Exhibit D [2]

103   INSTRUCTOR

68

484-246820-0

RECEIPT

Date Dec 27 19 83 No. 5415

Received From Wynona D. Quillen

Address 132 Page

For failed to stamps over payment for 10/18 3

eighty seven 00/100 —————— Dollars $ 87.80

ACCOUNT		HOW PAID	
	CASH	CHECK	MONEY ORDER
AMT. OF ACCOUNT	8700		
AMT. PAID	8700	8700	
BALANCE DUE	—0		

By LUCAS COUNTY WELFARE DEPT.

All that changed one cold December afternoon. The academy class had just completed a three-mile run. Jimi and others were in the gym learning defensive maneuvers and self-defense. Suddenly the class was stopped, and five cadets' names were called out including Jimi's. They were escorted home and their gear including uniforms taken from them right away.

It turned out that one of the female cadets, who was on ADC (Aid for Dependent Children) received her October check very late. Instead of cashing the check, she went to a training officer and asked him if it was okay to cash that last check. She too would have been cut off automatically if she did not reapply for ADC.

The story goes that the training officer told her not to cash the check and took the check to the chief of police. The chief told the training officer to advise the cadet to send the check back. He also instructed the trainer to investigate everybody in the academy to determine if anyone else had used any form of aid since entering the academy. Jimi and the four other cadets had received their October benefits in the form of food stamps, ADC, or a combination of the two and used them. They all had the same assumption that they would be cut off automatically and that receiving a check meant they were eligible for the benefit.

The chief of police fired the five who had received this federal aid early in October and used it since they had been on the city's payroll since the academy began in September. The police chief then turned the matter over to the grand jury for possible criminal prosecution. The grand jury declined to indict the five because of the small amounts involved. Unfortunately, the five cadets were told that they had no legal standing to fight their firing because they were still on probation and probationary cadets did not have legal recourse in such matters.

The firing haunted the boy and even today still bothers him from time to time, especially when he sees his friends who completed the academy and have made it to sergeant and higher positions. The television and print news media dogged Jimi and his colleagues for two weeks before resting their case with the following printout, dated December 29, 1983 (see exhibit E).

With the unsavory taste of injustice still in his mouth Jimi sought employment in the private sector. He soon landed a job as a manager/director of housekeeping, at a local mini-mall marketplace. The Portside Festival Marketplace offered everything from gift shops, selling fashion, jewelry and spices to specialty chocolate shops. The eateries were many - from fast food such as the steak express, gyros, pizzas, and salads to a regular big-time seafood restaurant. A boardwalk and an amphitheater-style court attracted romantic couples and religious groups that performed gospel music on weekends at the portside.

City of Cincinnati

Civil Service Commission
Richard E. Guggenheim, *Chairman*
John A. West, *Vice Chairman*
V. Daniel Radford, *Member*

Room 215, City Hall
801 Plum Street
Cincinnati, Ohio 45202
Phone (513) 352-2400

Robert W. Burnett, *Secretary*

September 19, 1989

Jimi Dillon
1751 Ottawa Drive
Toledo, Ohio   43606

Dear Mr. Dillon:

This letter is to inform you of your status in the Police Recruit
selection process.

Your placement on the eligible list is #31. However, you did not
rank high enough to be considered for the October, 1989 Police
Recruit class. Your name will remain on the current eligible list
until it expires on September 11, 1990. If an additional class is
chosen from this list, you will be considered for employment as a
Police Recruit.

Thank you for your interest in employment with the City of
Cincinnati.

Sincerely,

Robert W. Burnett

Robert W. Burnett
Director of Personnel

RWB:CC:bw

Exhibit G

114

The boy was responsible for interviewing, hiring and quickly training
seventy-one applicants who helped him run his department. The atmosphere was
beautiful, the job was tough, but Jimi liked it. The marketplace had been
modeled after successful ones, such as the one in Norfolk, Virginia and Boston,
Massachusetts; and even one built after it in Detroit, Michigan and Cincinnati,
Ohio. The marketplace opened during a time of economic crises in the whole
country, perhaps, the world over. It was also planned poorly - location with less
business in the city to support it and a city that did not market it property. The

Portside Festival Marketplace, bombarded with these factors and other mitigating factors the boy dare not mention here, caused the marketplace to shut down. Jimi's department was shut down and everybody was laid off - including him. Jimi had this job from March 1984 to January 1986 and was laid off along with everyone else.

The boy began looking for another job in his field as a law enforcement officer, but found a shop driver's position in March 1986. He took the job to continue feeding his family, while he continued to seek his career job. While still working as a shop truck driver, for a mechanical plumbing company, Jimi applied for the position of deputy sheriff a second time. On both occasions he was denied employment, which actions he believes were discriminatory. He filed a case of discrimination with the local OCRC - (Ohio Civil Rights Commission) (see exhibit F).

CITY OF **TOLEDO** OHIO

CIVIL SERVICE COMMISSION
ONE GOVERNMENT CENTER, SUITE 1920
TOLEDO, OHIO 43604
(419) 245-1500

COMMISSION MEMBERS
WILLIAM M. CONNELLY
President
FRAN DARCY
JOHN L. LANDRY

PEG WALLACE, *Chief*
Selection and Evaluation

February 27, 1990

Jimi D. Dillon, Sr.   I.D.# <u>0050</u>
1751 Ottawa Drive
Toledo, OH 43606

Dear Mr. Dillon:

At the February 22, 1990 meeting of the Toledo Civil Service
Commission, your appeal of the rejection of your Correctional
Officer application was submitted. After a careful review of the
information presented, the Commission determined that your
credentials do meet the minimum requirements for this classifi-
cation. Therefore, your application was approved and your name
will be forwarded to the Toledo House of Corrections for
consideration.

If you have any questions concerning this matter, please contact
Crystal Dixon of this office at 245-1500.

Sincerely,

Peg Wallace

Peg Wallace, Chief
Selection and Evaluation

PW:CYD:mw

crctacpl.pw

73

Jimi felt that if this case went to trial, he had enough evidence to win easily with a jury. But the respondent quickly employed a destructive tactic that would divide Jimi's family - pitching family members against one another. Jimi's wife had a younger sister. Her husband was a deputy sheriff at the time he charged the respondent with discrimination. Jimi was told that candidates had to have a bachelor's degree, correction experience and veteran's status, but his brother-in-law was admitted to the class without these credentials. Although Jimi told the recruiter that he had an associate degree and a private police-training certificate in law enforcement, he was still refused employment. Jimi's brother-in-law became an instant scapegoat to be used against him.

Jimi had been an associate minister in the Christian faith since 1975. His faith strengthened him to endure his previous calamities and this one was no exception. The in-law started getting static from superior officers. In fact he was told bluntly that he would not be taking a special class for promotion, because Jimi had stated that the Deputy did not have a bachelor's degree or military or corrections background. Yet he was hired in the 19th class, while the boy was told he had to have those same credentials. Jimi's brother-in-law was told if he did not make Jimi back off, he might not get the special training to work in the courts and could lose his job. The brother-in-law now a deputy began to complain to his wife that the boy's actions against the department were causing problems for him. He said his job was being threatened.

The deputy's wife began to call Jimi's wife to convince him to back off. She didn't say so in those exact words, but her implication was clear. Jimi's wife was very concerned and always considered her family ties as paramount. Neither she nor Jimi wanted any hard feelings between her sister's family and theirs, so Jimi withdrew his right to sue at that time, to save the families. The brother in-law received that special training and his promotion at last. Jimi believes he would have won that case and gotten his career job or some money in a settlement to rectify the wrongs done to him.

After the boy withdrew his right to sue the Lucas County Sheriffs Department because of the rift it would have created between the families, he then understood why the old Negro slaves sang the old spiritual, "nobody knows the troubles I've seen, nobody knows but Jesus."

Chapter 22

When it Rains, It Pours

After this terrible blow and the setback to Jimi's career and future, he didn't give up hope. Due to his incessant search for a career job, he learned of a police-recruiting test being administered by the City of Cincinnati, Ohio. He made the contact and were scheduled to be tested. Cincinnati is about four hours normal driving time from Toledo. The boy made four trips to meet all requirements of the testing processes. He had spent thirty-two plus hours on the unfriendly highways, in all sorts of weather, with great anxiety. He waited impatiently for the test result to be received.

A letter arrived one September evening, in his mailbox (see exhibit G). Words can't express his exhilaration and excitement. He was almost sure this time he was going to get his career job. After all, he heard that the city was going to hire about fifty officers. Even though he knew that about a thousand plus people took the test, he felt his overall test score would place him in the elite fifty to be selected for the next academy. The first class hired only about thirty cadets.

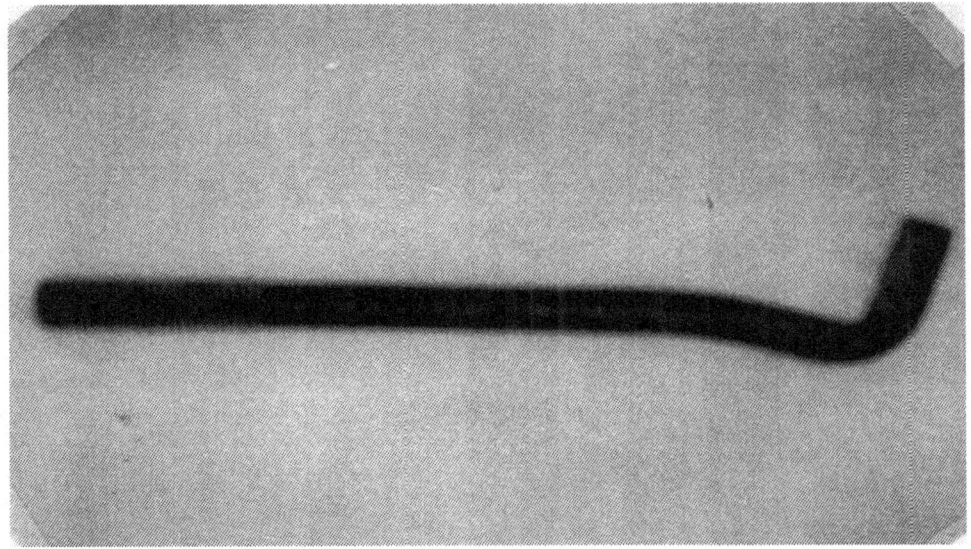

After about a year of impatiently waiting to be called or written, Jimi received from a second-hand source a bit of information that the city of Cincinnati had indeed hired its second police recruit class of about forty cadets.

He was furious that he was not among those selected. He rushed to the phone and called the Civil Service Commission of Cincinnati. The answer he got was unsatisfactory. The lady told him to put his grievance in writing and told him where and to whom it should be addressed.

Jimi's letter (see exhibit H) to the Civil Service Commission was in essence a protest of the way he had been treated and denied a place in the police academy. He wrote that if indeed a test is administered by the Civil Service Commission, then the selection of candidates for hire should be based solely on the individual candidates' qualifications and ranking of the total testing scores.

Jimi sent an angry second letter in response to a letter he had received from the Civil Service Commission of Cincinnati. It stated that even though he had scored high on the qualifying list (see exhibits J K), the city of Cincinnati gave the chief of police the authority to pick individuals off the qualifying list as he saw fit.

City of Cincinnati

Department of Safety
Division of Police

310 Ezzard Charles Drive
Cincinnati, Ohio 45214
513-352-3536

Lawrence E. Whalen
Police Chief

July 13, 1990

Jimi Dillon
33 Kenilworth Avenue
Toledo, OH 43608

Dear Mr. Dillon,

The Cincinnati Police Recruiting Unit is in receipt of your letter of June 29, 1990, pertaining to your placement status in the Police Recruit Selection Process.

The Recruiting Unit does not handle the notifying of the applicant of his/her placement status. The Cincinnati Civil Service Personnel Office is responsible for making notifications. Therefore, this matter has been forwarded to Ms. Carole Callahan, Supervising Personnel Analyst in the office of the Cincinnati Civil Service Personnel. Ms. Callahan has informed me that she will be contacting you by telephone or letter in regards to your inquiry.

Please contact me if I can be of further assistance.

Sincerely,

Sgt. Dwight Jorden
Recruiting Unit
CINCINNATI POLICE DIVISION
310 Ezzard Charles Drive
Cincinnati, OH 45214
(513) 352-2971

DJ/kmj

Exhibit J

117

Equal Opportunity Employer

City of Cincinnati

Civil Service Commission
Richard E. Guggenheim, *Chairman*
John A. West, *Vice Chairman*
V. Daniel Radford, *Member*

Room 215. City Hall
801 Plum Street
Cincinnati. Ohio 45202
Phone (513) 352-2400

Robert W. Burnett, *Secretar*

July 19, 1990

Mr. Jimi D. Dillon Sr.
33 Kenilworth Avenue
Toledo, Ohio 43608

Dear Mr. Dillon:

This letter is in response to your recent correspondence to Police Chief Larry Whalen concerning the position of Police Recruit.

Your statements are correct that you did not place high enough in the selection process to be considered for the October, 1989 Police Recruit class and that you would be considered for any additional class taken from the eligible list.

However, under Ohio State Civil Service Law, the appointing authority may consider three candidates for each position vacancy. After being considered for four vacancies and not being appointed, the candidate may be eliminated from further consideration.

The position of Police Recruit in the City of Cincinnati is highly competitive and the process is one of comparison. Not being selected for a position does not necessary mean that you are not qualified, but rather that the qualifications of others exceeded yours. Regretfully, after considering you and others for four of the Police Recruit vacancies, the Police Division declined to appoint you to the Spring, 1990 Police Recruit class. You were notified of this decision earlier this year.

I apologize for any misunderstanding and thank you for your interest in employment with the Cincinnati Police Division.

Sincerely,

Carole Callahan

Carole Callahan
Supervising Personnel Analyst
Civil Service/Personnel

CC/cj

Exhibit K

118

Equal Opportunity Employer

Jimi's second letter accused the chief stealing, telling him how he felt cheated of his rightful place on the Cincinnati Police Force. He never received a response to his third and last letter.

Chapter 23

The Beat Goes On

"Complacency is a disease to the human mind and a handicap to human progress" says Jimi Dillon (JD). He knew he must find a job in his career field soon. He learned that the Toledo House of Corrections, a state-operated correctional facility was hiring. He immediately sent in his resume. He was hoping that this time he would be hired and he would finally begin his career ladder. This was in the summer of 1989. Instead of good news, the boy got a letter from civil service that he did not qualify to be hired as a correction officer. The boy was devastated and distraught. He immediately compiled a package of documents verifying his education and experience for the job which were comparable to people who were just completing training or who were to be trained on the job. He appealed the negative decision by the Civil Service Commission of Toledo, Ohio.

In February of 1990 Jimi received the following document (see exhibit L). Unfortunately by the time the boy received this letter, the position he wished to be considered for was already filled. He had to now decide whether to wait around for another year or two when another hiring might take place. He became desperate and began to daydream and fantasize.

In fact he wrote to himself that "life without fantasy is like being a dummy, which has not a mind. For we daydream many a time to keep our spirits high without reasoning immediately that what we dream of is often times impossible."

In spite of fantasies and daydreams we must face the realities of life with facts and our mind intact. Jimi reasoned that it was time to seek his career goals elsewhere in other cities, counties, and states.

Chapter 24

Seeking Southern Comfort

After all the disappointments Jimi encountered north of the border in Ohio, he decided it was time to head south. His wife had two sisters in Houston, Texas. She too had been laid off due to a company takeover. She left Jimi with their two sons and headed for Houston.

From early May to late June 1992 she found temporary employment. She managed to get an apartment, though empty, and all the utilities turned on. By late July she flew back to Toledo to get her family's household things. Her short stay away from her family was not without great suffering. Though she stayed with a sister upon her arrival in Houston, the buses did not run and there were no sidewalks in the neighborhood where she lived. In an effort to find quick employment, she had to walk long distances to catch a bus. She had never been used to walking. The sun was blistering hot. She recalls the sores and scars she developed while walking to and from the bus stops. She turned down many offers of a ride, because the area was isolated and she was afraid to ride with strangers.

She called her husband in Toledo frequently and asked him for monetary help and just a shoulder to cry on. The sister she lived with worked in the early morning and she could not take Jimi's wife job hunting. She survived her ordeal until July, when her family joined her in their new apartment. For her husband, it was a temporary move.

He was on vacation when he drove the family to Houston in a truck with most of their belongings. While in Houston, he soon found opportunity knocking at his door again…an opportunity in the career of his dream - law enforcement. Yes, here he went again!

Jimi learned that the Metropolitan Transit Authority police department was accepting applications. He quickly signed up for the test. In August of 1992, he took the test, and passed it. He also passed the physical and the background investigation, medical evaluation, and drug screening. After several trips to the Metro substation on the opposite side of town, the background investigation officer told Jimi on the phone that he had completed his investigation and did not find anything that would prevent him from being hired. However, the officer warned, a board did the actual hiring.

Metro headquarters advised Jimi that if and when the 1993 budget passed in December 1992, they would begin hiring new Metro officers in the new year. Anxiously, the boy took the whole new opportunity to heart and felt it was very exciting, even though he had to wait for the budget to pass and for the board to hire him.

He kissed his family and hurried back north. He worked two more weeks at his truck-driving job in Toledo, Ohio, and then he resigned that job knowing that soon the Metro police job would come through. He packed the rest of their belongings and put them in storage. He drove back to Houston in his old 1983 flat-back Cadillac Seville.

After arriving in Houston, he was sure that this time things would be different, compared to those terrible days in Ohio. He found temporary employment at a record storage warehouse. He did not like this sort of work because it reminded him of the heavy lifting he had done for five and a half years at the mechanical plumbing company in Toledo, so he left that job just three weeks after starting. He instead found a security officer job. Both of these jobs paid just a little above minimum wages at the time.

With patience running thin, he called the Metro administration office and asked to speak to someone in the personnel office. This was almost a year after his successful testing for the Metro job. The personnel lady, a Ms. Baker, told the boy to hold while she pulled his file.

The news from Ms. Baker stunned Jimi. According to Ms. Baker, Jimi's file showed that he had failed the written test in early August 1992. The boy screamed, 'That's a black lie!' He then apologized and gave her the details. He was one of a handful, out of about a hundred people who had passed the written test. In fact, he was third from the top of the passing list from which the Metro officer class was being hired. He gave Ms. Baker dates he took the physical agility test, the medical evaluation test and the background investigation. He even remembered the officer's name who did his background check.

Jimi was more than agitated, remembering all the disappointments he suffered in Ohio. Ms. Baker calmed him down from screaming and talking too fast, so that she could understand what had happened. She told Jimi to call her back in one week, so that she could talk to the police academy testers and responsible parties and find out what really happened. To her amazement, nobody actually told her what happened or who sent in the file saying that the boy had failed the written test. According to testing and recruitment rules, once a candidate fails any one aspect of the testing, that candidate is dropped automatically.

The fact that the boy was allowed to take all aspects of the testing was indeed proof that the boy had passed the written test. What really happened? To the best of Jimi's recollection, a white fellow who was first on the scene to take the written test had told him in a lengthy conversation that he had a close friend in the department and at the testing site. The fellow told the boy that his friend had promised him faithfully that if he passed the written test, he would do everything in his power to get him hired. But the young man failed the written test. How does the boy know? The name of the white fellow was right above Jimi's on the list of test takers. A failing grade was posted for him. He seemed upset at the end of the written test because he had failed.

The boy believes that someone in the police department switched that young white fellow's grade and his, passing the other man and failing him. The top twenty of the thirty-five who passed were going to be hired and Jimi was one of them.

After the boy finished talking to Ms. Baker, he contacted the EEOC in the Metro office, working with - and the boy believes for - Metro's interest. After weeks of so-called investigation into the complaint, the EEOC told Jimi that records could not be found besides that failed file in Ms. Baker's possession. He was told that he would have to reapply to the Metro police department and then take the next test if one came up.

Even a begging dog has pride. The boy realized that once again the axe of discrimination had been laid to the root of his tree - his career dream of becoming a law enforcement officer had once again been cut down. The boy believes that the two most important people in charge of the police academy at the time were responsible.

After all of the disappointments Jimi had suffered in trying to get career employment in America, he finally believed that often spoken heresy by most black Americans and some white Americans that discrimination and racism are part of the American tradition. Jimi admonishes all young people to fight for their right to the end. When is the end? The end is when you are satisfied that you have won the fight. The end is when you have fought a good fight and can't fight anymore!

For Jimi, now approaching fifty years old, he has fought a good fight and could fight for his career dream no more. He now works as a good juvenile corrections officer. But he wrote a poetic admonishment about the system in America.

YOU MADE IT TO THE TOP

So you made it to the top.
So what if you did
Are you satisfied you're there
Or are you there because they put you there
So you got there all by yourself, eh
But have you looked around you
And seen how many hands helped push you
You say it doesn't matter - I'm there.
Well don't be too contented
Because you are there.

You may have climbed up there,
To become self-conceited.
In which case you may fall
Sooner or later.
Or perhaps they put you there
As a scapegoat to fool your brothers,
That the system is equal to all
Don't be fooled
Unless you shine, and become outstanding,
Like your color.
You will deteriorate to fit the label... "Nigger,"
Which means dirt,
Or you'll shine like the setting sun,
And become lights unto your brothers.
So you made it to the top.
Show me how!

- JD -

PART III

Jimi Daniel Dillon

Chapter 25

The Environment Molded Man (EMM)

All humans are a by-product of their environment. The Kpelle Tribe, from whom the boy originates, is no exception. The greatest fear of an African tribal child is usually the first traumatic experience he witnesses or encounters. This proved true for the boy.

The boy loved water, from the day he was born, so he was told, until this day. He became very cautious of water when his first dog, whom we shall call "Spot," contracted a leach in the most important, and life-sustaining orifice of his body - his nostrils. Spot decided to lap some water out of a strange and slow-moving marshy pond. The boy's fear of a leach leaping into his nostrils stopped him from lapping water while on his knees or with his hand. He used a cup made of leaves from this point on in his life.

This pond was in a strange jungle where the boy and others went to hunt birds, squirrels, and the unexpected. There were creatures such as snakes, possums, ground hogs, etc. that sped off from their daytime feeding spots to avoid being chased by the dogs or even getting killed.

There was also a greater fear of the unexpected - the infamous leopard, tiger, or the fastest running cheetahs. African parents continually warned their children not to venture too far into the unknown jungle. The greatest and most common fear of all African villagers, both young and old, was poisonous snakes. As they traveled barefooted along the dusty roads to and from subsistence farming on a daily basis, the tall grass, marshes, forest floors of dried leaves, or even a well-grown rice farm presented a danger of poisonous snakes.

Perhaps, unlike those tribes who lived along the coastal regions of the great Atlantic Ocean and beside large rivers, the Kpelle were lucky to fish the river and lake banks through various means. They employed a technique of rotting some of their catches with salt. This process helped them keep some of those fish longer. Of course, no villagers had such modern necessities as refrigerators or freezers.

The Environment Molded Man (EMM), as the boy would like to call them, were ingenious when it came to test tasting strange foods - especially strange snakes they killed or found burned during their rice farm brush clearing. These snakes lived under the dried brushes and leaves that had been chopped down by the tribesmen to clear land for farming.

Since hunters had no way of identifying a burned snake, caught in a raging fire, the boy's father taught them to let their dog refuse the "nature cooked" snake; that meant the snake was too poisonous to be eaten by them. God gave the dog an acute 'scent sense". It was more valuable than the street smarts any city dweller could acquire.

In their quest for survival, the boy believes that the tribal villagers ignorantly, yet slowly, poisoned their own bodies. They ate maggot infested meats. One could actually see the dead maggots floating on top of the soups or in their fried greens, etc. In fact, the more rotten the meat and the more odorous it was, the better it appealed to their sense of smell and taste. It made them sick too, but seldom. The children were often infested with stomach/intestinal worms. The villagers also knew the right herbs to boil to get rid of those blood-sucking maggots.

The tribal children also ate water bugs or large water roaches, bamboo worms, and certain tree grubs and vegetable grub varieties. Bats, all species of the rat family, and lizards both big and small, including iguana, made up part of the jungle dweller's diet. The boy's tribes and neighbors were more concerned with survival and health issues were secondary, if they were considered at all.

The tribe also ate most large spiders, but not the tarantula. One had bitten the boy while he played "hide and seek" with his friends. The tarantula was hidden in the dried banana leaves. As the boy hid and hugged the dry leaves, the spider bit and stung him on his chest. He ran to his dad crying and told him what happened. His dad ran to the scene with his machete, thinking he had been bitten by a snake. He killed the spider, then got some herbal jelly from a swamp tree and treated the wounded areas. He showed the boy the hairy dead bug, warning him never to contend with a live one, even a baby one, except in a life and death situation.

As the hurd bird feeds its baby with chewed and digested leaves, the tribal mothers fed their children with grounded and boiled "monkey leaves." The tree is regarded as a source of food for babies as rich as breast milk. This was often used as a substitute if the mother had insufficient breast milk or when the mother was ill and she could not breast-feed.

After the boy's migration to the United States, he became startled, as he drove along streets and highways of America, and saw dead animals on the roadsides in season. He reflected back to the days that those dead animals would have made great eating, especially when the family's traps failed to yield their prey. Certainly those "road kills" would have been thought of as 'luck" or providence of the spirits, or God's given grace. In the jungle there were no roads or cars to produce "road kill."

The excitement and anticipation of spotting a bird's nest in the lower branches of shrubbery or a tree were still fresh on the boy's mind when he immigrated to the United States. The excitement of reaching into the nest and plucking out the eggs for roasting as a snack still haunted the boy. The baby birds from those nests became pets for the tribal children for the first hour. When they became too weak, by the treatment of rough human hands or from hunger, the boy and his siblings then killed and roasted them as snacks or delicacies. They even ate burnt palm kernel oil, which is loaded with cholesterol. The natives did not know anything about healthy foods.

A sign on Highway 223 out of Sandusky, Ohio, reads "Where Man Bites Dog." At first, those words tickled Jimi. And he laughed because they sounded silly. But that thought and phrase soon began to trouble him. A feeling of dread suddenly came over him. He realized that it was so ironic because he had just been thinking how they (his family) ate Puddy. Puddy was their dog that had died after being bitten by a snake. Yes, his tribe ate dogs, as did so many other West African primitive tribes. That dog was a ready source of protein and meat, one that the boy's family did not have to hunt down and kill.

This was the case with all animals that were raised and bred by the tribe. Then some of the tribesmen were educated in the "Western Principle", that man does not eat his best friend - his dog, or other pets. What bothered Jimi most was the brutal way in which a dog was killed for food. The poor animal was taken behind the farm hut, where it had grown from a puppy. It had lived there with the family, his best friends. There the dog was clubbed over the top of its head until it fell helpless, bled, and died. The boy believes the killing was even more hideous and painful for the bigger dogs.

The boy had heard of accounts where the poor animal staggered to its feet and tried to escape from its attacker. This was usually after it had been struck several times across the head with a club. It ended up dying a slow and painful death. Please forgive us, the boy pleads. We were primitive and did not know any better - that man does not kill his best friend for food - especially by the method they used to do so. Jimi can only guess that it was that instinct of primitive man, to hunt that way. The clubbing of animals for food was the accepted method before men learned to trap, or use bow and arrow, or spears to kill for their meat, fish, birds, snakes, etc.

Nature is bad! Nature is good! Nature can be wickedly disastrous in one place, yet she can be compassionately blissful in another. So is the former case for the village jungle farmer. Who will teach the West of the failed farms of the jungle farmer? Who will teach you brethren of his immeasurable pains and agonies? Look on here of the picture of a failed farm and thrust your eyes on what would have been his daily bread!

The West cries of starvation, poverty, and hardships in the cities! You haven't seen anything yet! In the years the farm failed, the jungle native ate "greens on greens" without salt, pepper, or oil. If only he knew miracles, he could supplement his diet with wild berries and fruits of the jungle. He could only hope of yams (wild roots) that the jungle would yield or a green breadfruit dangling from its tree. His fate was now in a neighbor, whose farm may have blossomed bountifully. His family must labor on that neighbor's farm for a meager portion of that harvest to sustain his family momentarily. The West has not seen comparable hardships to this degree?

Jimi recalls how his grandpa would break the chickens' legs to keep them from scratching the newly planted rice from the ground. In the evening, he would reset their legs and in a few days the chickens would heal and be normal again. By this time the grain would have set in the soil well and was covered properly. The chickens could no longer see the seeds and try to scratch them out of the ground for food. Other methods of protecting the rice farm included the use of slings with shots (stones) to keep or drive the pesky rice birds away. Jimi wrote this poem about the problem.

Rice Bird

Rice bird, rice bird
Flutter of wings in harmony.
You'd think it's Niagara Falls
With their melodious song.
They sing in deceit
Whilst they converge in swarm.
To spurt the early harvest of Rice
Or diminish the late harvest
Robbing the poor farmer
Of his just due
For his hard labor.
The jungle farmer dreads them
The village youths loathe them - with hatred.
Youths are forced to work - twice as hard
Slinging the birds away - rain or shine
January through December
Than any other season
In the twelve months of the year.

- JD -

By August most farmers completed weeding the young rice stalks. Children were responsible for guarding the rice's growth. They were left sitting on makeshift raised platforms to guard the rice against birds and other edibles such as ground peas (peanuts) which were guarded against squirrels. "Lown" is the ground squirrel's Kpelle name. Like it's name suggest, it is a low-down creature when it comes to destroying the harvest. The planting season seemed to have brought out the worst of nature's creatures and they made the jungle youths work twice as hard to protect their daily bread.

Chapter 26
Beauty and the Seer

It is said, "beauty is in the eye of the beholder." In the young-village life of this boy, beauty was a pure, natural look, as opposed to today's formula of clothing, make-up, and physical upkeep of the body. The boy had a cousin, his father's sister's daughter. She was so light-skinned you could not tell her from a white person. The niece had a straight nose on a small face, compared to many Africans who have a wide nose. She was petite, with deep blue piercing eyes with a catwalk. She seldom smiled, though she had nothing to hide for she had a perfect set of white teeth. It was the color of her skin that aroused the boy's curiosity. He asked his dad why she was so light-skinned compared to her mother who was very dark-skinned. His Dad simply said that people are made differently and he would begin to understand, as he grew older.

In contrast to his cousin, her older brother, Ghan-Khay, was equally handsome, but he was as dark as their mother. He was very quiet, unmarried, probably in his early twenties when he took the boy on his first hunt. They were looking for food supplements as are most indigenous Africans.

They still lack the technology today to grow enough of the needed foods. They hunted for small game - birds, squirrels, etc. that forage for food in daylight. Most big game only came out at night, at sunset, or in the early dawn. On the hunt they found only yams, a root plant similar to the cassava root plant. The boy also found a leopard snail at the end of the hunt on their way home. The snail was so called by this name because its black and golden-brown spots are arranged in broken rings or rosettes, resembling the leopard. This particular snail and the hard-shell medium turtles were common in the jungles of West Africa. The lanky six or seven-year-old was very excited. To him this was a successful hunt in his early life.

Then tragedy struck! About six months after the hunt, the boy learned that his favorite cousin had died suddenly. He was told that Ghan-Khay had a short illness, with fever and headache, and had died unexpectedly. Ironically, the boy recalls that his beautiful, almost white niece (though the boy had never seen a white person before) had died of similar circumstances. The only difference was that she had always been sickly.

Then came the terrible revelation that cousin Ghan-Khay had been involved in a tribal secret society called Leopardess. Very little was known of the Leopardess (Koliisuu) Society. According to the boy's father, in this secret society individual members would sacrifice a blood relative, especially their child. How it was done, the boy doesn't know.

The sacrifice was to kill a relative initially after joining through witchcraft. Failure to do so would bar members from killing other people's animals or livestock after they changed to a leopard through witchcraft at certain times of the year. Did Jimi's cousin take him hunting to sacrifice him? He doesn't know. It is said that Ghan-Khay had not met his obligations of the sacrifice. He had not killed a close relative through witchcraft. He had changed into a leopard at night and went after another's livestock to kill and eat it as a leopard does. He was shot fatally, not his person, but in the leopard form. As the leopard died slowly, so did he on his dying bed with blood coming out of his skin in his chest, under his arm, and from his nostrils. That's what the boy was told.

How such acts are accomplished, Jimi does not know. Witchcraft and voodoo were practiced in his little Liberian town of Gbunontaa (pronounced *Bu-non-town*), but he left for the city before his mind was old enough to comprehend witchcraft. But he will tell you of one experience, and you be the judge of any witchcraft.

Jimi has a younger sister. She was born a very beautiful child. She could have won beauty contest, had she been born on the other side of the world. She was born with natural braids, a sign to West African villagers that she would be someone special.

At about a week old, this very strong child took on a strange sickness. She would just scream off and on in spurts. The town medicine man, Tolon came to the family's hut and did all he could do herbally. About twenty degrees east of the boy's house stood a giant cotton tree. The tree never bears cotton in its season. It also stood near and over a graveyard. It was said that a big snake, to which other villagers sacrificed other people's children, inhabited that tree from time to time. The snake would make a strange "begging" sound, like that of a bat— "gong, gong, gong…" throughout the night. This strange cry by the snake was interpreted to mean "give me, give me, give me," and was usually followed by the death of an infant in the town. But on that misty, dark night as the snake cried out, "gong, gong, gong" before the middle of the night, Jimi's father took the crying and pale infant outside, with his wife crying, the boy and other siblings following. The father lifted the crying child into the air, and would shout, "you out there who is trying to take the life of my young baby, I don't believe I've done you any wrong. My child here, God gives her to me. If you take her life, I swear I will not rest until I take your life, and those you love. Even if I have to go to the end of the world. And believe me I know where to go to find out who you are."

Jimi shivered at hearing these angry remarks by his distraught father. At the very moment the boy's father uttered those words, the snake stop crying out its eerie, "gong, gong, gong"! At that instant, the boy's sister also stopped crying. And her fever broke. The child became well. She is alive today. Was it witchcraft? You be the judge.

It should be noted here that the boy's father spoke seven tribal languages or dialects. This led the boy to believe that his father would know where to go for revenge, had his daughter died through witchcraft. He knew where to find the right voodoo man or doctor for his revenge. The one other incident Jimi can document about what some may call witchcraft, voodoo or a mystery to the indigenous West African, involved a tribal chief named Gbono Gboivie. He governed a large town called "Gbatelala" in Bong County, Liberia. This town was more developed than most of the surrounding towns. It had a one-lane dusty auto road leading through it, from a larger town called Totota, one of the missionary stations in Liberia. The population of Gbatelala may have been 300 or more. Most West African towns in that part of the world had less than 100 adults living within. Here Jimi experienced a miracle that some have attributed to witchcraft or voodoo. Chief Gboivie had some catfish in a river downtown. The townsfolk called them his personal catfish although they lived in a free running creek. There were about four catfish. Whenever anyone went to the creek's bank and whistled, the catfish would come out. Anyone was allowed to feed them. They were in no special holding tank or cage or fenced in. They would come out when whistled to, eat any food given them, roam freely in the shallow areas of the running creek, and go back into their hole in the creek's bank.

It was said that if anyone would try feeding the catfish with foreign or poisonous foods - berries, grubs, worms, etc. - the fish would not bite or touch them. Young people even tried fishing out those catfish, but could not catch them with a hook, no matter what bait they used. On one rainy night a young man in his early twenties took a net, shovel, and a digger or trowel and dug out the catfish from their burrows in the creek's bank. As he made his way to town, one of the catfish snagged him on the finger with its fin. The young man died before he could reach home with his stolen catfish. Other villagers found him lying beside the road with the catfish scattered in the ditches dying too. They all died at the same precise time - man and fish. Was it catfish venom that killed the young man or witchcraft or voodoo? You be the judge. This was Jimi's last experience with hearing about witchcraft before the experience of civilization.

Jimi's first experience in trading when he was boy about six or seven years old, the Liberian government had mandated that all villages trade with larger villages or towns. This mandatory trading was done in the barter system. Since most natives did not have currency they traded goods with each other.

In this form of trading, some got less value for their "blood and sweat" products and some got more for products they sweated less to produce. The latter products were simple "seasonal", and hard to find or the demand of such product was high, but less in quality. The villagers often had the "blood and sweat" produced goods. Such wee palm oil, palm cabbage, palm kernel nut oil, etc. Had they known what the boy knows now, they would have made a killing with the palm butter that was always destroyed. They did not know the processing and storage of it. So they lost a great business. Today palm butter is sold all over the world. The boy knows, because he eats it. And it is very expensive to buy here in America, where the boy lives. The villagers sold such demanded products such as avocados, papaya, pineapples, mangoes, African plums, wild cherries, kiwis, sweet mushrooms, just to name a few.

They in turn got unequal trade values. They got such goods as salt, tobacco, washing soap bars, which was more of a quarter bar, smoke fish, cans of sardines, etc. and eventually clothing. On one of these trips, the boy and others went to the missionary compound. They had heard of its beauty (semi modern architecture), a lawn and dust walkway. It also had a water tank on a wooden frame tower in the back of the one "squared" flat house. Other than old catalogue pictures, the boy saw his first white humans. It excited him so much that he carefully walked over to the little boy.

He was riding his tricycle and had stopped in curiosity (too) to see the brave African boy came so close. The boy touched the golden white hair of the little white child. It was starry and tough fooling the boy, who had thought it, was soft as palm leaves flax, used to make personal baskets.

The boy quickly touched the child's arm to feel his soft-looking skin. It felt no different from his. The boy smiled at the child, who began to call his mother. He probably sensed some fear since the African boy was so bold. Jimi believes the missionary mother may have been watching the whole incident from their one-story house window. She hurriedly answered her child's call. She came out and immediately escorted her son into the house, tricycle and all. The boy's exhilaration had soared when he saw the white lady come out of the house. She was tall, and yes, beautiful as the catalogues portrayed. The boy does not believe she saw him as a threat to her son but gave the parental "you are safe" touch and talk to her son before taking him into the house. The boy left with the others. He could not wait to tell his folks what he had experienced. On other visits the mother took the child into the house, every time the boy and his entourage came to watch them.

This was especially when the child was riding his tricycle or his little red wagon. The boy did not know what a wagon was then. When the white family was eating, they would close the front door to keep the boy and others from watching them each lunch.

By the way, this was the first time the boy had seen a lawn. It was cut and trimmed. The boy thought to himself, "how beautiful the big city must look." But to the boy's surprise, when he went to the big city of Monrovia, he did not see many lawns in the public sections of the city. The boy wished most to see a motorcar, for he had heard how fast they moved, and they were pretty, especially the missionary cars, compared to trucks. The boy's description of the little white boy's and his mom's skin was third in the group of his new and exciting experiences.   They looked pale yellowish, an observation the boy got from harvesting the bamboo borer (larvae) or the weevil larvae of the West African swamp bamboo plant trees - commonly called "Killie-Collod" (bamboo worm). Their skin reminded him of the bamboo worm's skin.

The only three colors known to most jungle village dwellers are black, red, and white. They associate every other colors known in the modem and scientific world to those three colors.   They called all Caucasians white people, even Asians and Puerto Ricans.

The boy as a youth had first used his finger to brush his teeth.   Then the family used charcoal. As the children got older, they used the bamboo or rattan stick as a toothbrush.   Once he spotted the little white boy with his toothbrush, brushing his teeth.   At the time the boy did not know what the little white boy was doing. He had never seen a Western-made toothbrush. When he got home, he told his father what the little white boy was doing. The white child had a red piece of stick in his mouth going from side to side.   His father told him that it was the white man's bamboo stick, used to brush their teeth. When the boy went to live in the city, he saw a real toothbrush for the first time up close.

Using and describing the sense of taste in the village, all foods were described in two taste groups. The sweet group was anything not bitter, a sugar taste. All fruits that tasted like sugar was considered sweet, so was salt taste. All food seasoned with salt properly was said to be sweet as well. The bitter taste group was anything unsavory. Generally a sour fruit or other food was simply described *as kang-kang* (tangy), like lime, lemon, or vinegar.

Unlike in English or other languages, the villagers describe peppers as hot, medium or mild. The tribal people of the boy's village associated hot pepper with a "hurting" pepper.   The Kpelle word "*sholii*" simply means, "hurting", hence one would say "Gee-ion-ah Shohi", meaning the pepper burns or is hot. In fact all painful conditions associated with the body are described as "*Sholii*," including words for headache, painful joint, or painful stomach.

Chapter 27

Reflections

While in his jungle village, the boy seldom had the privilege of getting a second, third, or fourth hand clothing catalogs. His thoughtful father brought them back, when he returned from one of his *"plotou"* or "man-soldier" duties. Man-soldier was a short and an easy way of saying "militia man" soldier. Yes, apart from performing Tubman governments *plotou* chores, the boy's father was also the most prominent militiaman in the village. These militiamen performed soldier-type duties without pay or any form of compensation. Although their uniforms were furnished free initially, individuals had to pay for their second set.

What amazed the boy and some of his siblings was the fact that they saw the Kweh children (white and black) in those catalogs sit on the beds - with feet and shoes on the bed while they put on their shoes. They often wondered if there were mud and dirt in America. The Kweh kid's shoes always looked clean and new. The boy envied them and wished he could be in their place. After he went to civilization, he realized after some education that there is mud and dirt in America. He later understood that the pictures were all a "sales pitch": to get the Kweh parent to buy the shoes for their children.

Today some children do keep their shoes clean enough to put them on their beds before they put them on. Unlike the first white missionary the boy saw eating, (they hid themselves from view while eating), the boy's villagers ate with whomever was visiting at the time of a meal, usually lunch or dinner. Breakfast was unusual, except for leftover foods. Sometimes it was oranges from the back perimeter of their village hut or a banana picked and put in the hut's attic to ripen. Most villagers were related in some fashion, so it was not so hard to entertain a so-called stranger to "hand eat" with them from the same bowl or pan.

The boy's father developed a strategy to use when strangers ate with him and his family. On one of his *"plotou"* trips, he had obtained a large "military type" tablespoon. He named this spoon *"wand-par"* meaning "stranger killer" in the Kpelle dialect. He jokingly told his family that whenever he invited a stranger to eat, he got out his *"wandpar"*, so he could eat more than the unsuspecting stranger. He'd usually give the stranger a regular tablespoon to eat with. Most village dinners were served by the light of a fire or kerosene lantern, so there was not much light for the stranger to notice the father's larger *"wand-par"*.

Chapter 28

The Invasion of the Body Shrinkers

While the boy has been in the States, he has surprised quite a few friends and co-workers with his rapid eating. Some have commented, "Damn Jimi, your food is not going to run away!" Jimi would smile quickly and slow his eating at times. What Americans do not know is that in the boy's village, all children shared food from one bowl at dinner or suppertime. Most village children did not eat a regular breakfast, as in the West. Children eating out of one bowl and with their hands had to eat fast, if they wanted to get full or even get their fair share. This was especially a problem for the smaller children, if the older one was being inconsiderate of the smaller siblings.

As long as two or more shared that bowl, there was competition, sometimes so fierce that some of the younger children cried. They cried because the older children had eaten most of the food faster and had bigger hands. They felt cheated. Mom or Dad had to intervene sometimes to slow or stop the bigger children from eating most of the foods. Sometimes the remainder in the bottom of the pan was seized and given to the younger siblings who were crying foul.

At other times when the food was finished, Mom or Dad would console the crying child with a piece of their meat or some food from their bowl or pan. The adults ate together too, from one bowl. They, of course, were considerate of each other and they tried to divide the portions equally.

The boy believes that most children and youth of the West African jungle tribes became immune to bacterial food poisonings because of their eating habits. They ate food after it had set overnight un-refrigerated. These spoiled leftovers had two or more children eating with their hands out of one bowl or pan. There were no refrigerators to keep the food cool.

The results of eating such foods were varied. Some villagers pulled live, round tapeworms out of their anus or some passed worms in their stools when they became too infested. The boy suffered such an experience. He felt something tickling in his rectum. He ran from the house where a dubbing party (a new hut being dubbed or plastered with soft mud) was being held. He went behind the banana bushes and pulled what seemed to be some form of thread from his anus. It was a live worm..

Shocked at the sight, he ran back and told his father what had happened. The most common symptom of tapeworms was a form of viral fever, followed by stomachache and a belly full of gas. Although the parents knew the kind of herbs to pick and boil for the sick child or children drink it, the herbs made them pass dead or at times not-so-dead worms in their stool. The herbs did make them well again, at least until a poor and hard harvest struck again. In this poor tribal society "expired dated foods" were relished by people who were on the brink of dying. They ate the bad, out-dated foods or died of starvation - it was that simple. Now the boy's American wife understands why he loves to eat leftovers. He was taught not to waste anything edible.

Chapter 29

The Stealth Suckers Attack

In addition to intestinal worms, tribal youths were often attacked by arachnids. These "snatchers," as they were called, were organisms of three kinds: chiggers, chinks and flies. A chigger, a tiny red larva of a certain arachnid, is a parasite, a member of the sand flea family. It is usually found on certain bush-dwelling animals. Its bites cause extreme itching. The larva develops into an egg sac the size of a BB gun pellet. It matures and hatches in a short time, if the egg sac is not removed from under the skin of its victim.

Another bloodsucker of the villagers was called the chinks, resembling a swallow bird bug, only smaller. When it is squashed, it smells like stale ammonia. These particular bugs infested the grass straw of the homemade mattresses of the villagers. The bugs bite only while the unsuspecting victim sleeps. If the infestation were bad enough, the victim would not sleep well and would arise sluggish and tired in the morning.

The third bug of prey was a maggot from a certain fly. These blood-sucking flies would attack an open sore to suck and lay an egg or would bite the victim until a small cut was made into which they would then deposit an egg. These flies also laid their eggs on "wet" beds - beds in which kids with weak bladders or wetting dreams slept.

As a young boy, someone usually would take Jimi near the banana bushes, where he urinated in the daytime. In his dream, he would begin to pee and then jump awake, realizing he was lying in bed. He would then wake up his grandpa or grandma to take him outside. By then it was too late; his rectangular "mud slab bed" was already damp enough to attract the bloodsucking flies in the morning or during the day. The bed was built with sticks about a foot from the main floor and attached to an inside wall of the hut. It was filled with clay soil from a creek's bank, and plastered with clay. These maggots would bury themselves in the wet mud bed and find their victim at night from sensing body heat. The boy's grandmother usually got rid of them by boiling certain herbs and pouring the boiling liquid all over the mud bed. At times of heavy infestation she would replaster the mud bed with heavy clay. It usually buried the menacing suckers until they died.

Tribal children swam a lot, sometimes in muddy waters. They did not have soap to use most of the time, so it was not a matter of filthiness that caused the boy and his siblings to contact chiggers. Once the boy got so infested that the chiggers attacked the skin of his penis. All this was due to ignorance on the part of a society that did not have education at its disposal about preventing and curing diseases. The boy's villagers were unlearned, yet through God's miracles of providence, they were able to tame and conquer many diseases and sicknesses before the West developed cures and prevention.

The boy's father learned how kerosene and snuff, a tobacco powder mixture, could cure and keep the chiggers away from his children. And so he used it well. It cured all his children and other children of the village who were affected. Some of the diseases the villagers did not have cures for included most eye problems such as trachoma and glaucoma. His grandfather suffered from both glaucoma and severe toothaches, which contributed to earaches. He also suffered from heart mummers and sinus problems. The boy himself, besides intestinal worms and the external suckers, suffered what is known today as "piles" or hemorrhoids. The village herbalist knew the right plants that cured the boy's condition.

Chapter 30

The Sacrifice of Blessings

The boy remembers at one time, that a sacrifice was made. The purpose of the ritual was for the new farm of that year to prosper and yield bountifully. The sacrifice was to appease the spirits of dead relatives to bless and help the family to produce rice and other farm crops bountifully. This was done, usually following a year of poor and unproductive farming or if an older member of the farming family passed on to the afterlife.

This particular sacrifice included a white chicken probably a rooster; pure white rice or fresh rice from the previous farm before any was cooked for eating; and newly made palm oil from fresh palm nuts. Decayed nuts oil was made and used regularly, but not for a sacrifice. No unnatural ingredients such as salt were used. If there was no fresh oil, only joya, a plain clear soup type, was used. All parts of the chicken were used, including the cleaned intestine, the head with its crown, and the feet, which had been cleaned. The sacrifice was offered early in the morning before sunrise and before any member of the family could use the latrine.

The cooked soup was poured directly over the bowl of cooked rice. The words of blessing, employing the names of the deceased, were repeated, then all members of the family would answer with an affirmation, such as "Amen." Before anyone would taste the food, some was thrown at the base of a special banana or plantain tree.

The banana tree is said to have had special qualities; hence it was used as a sacrifice tree and treated with reverence and respect. Children were not allowed to eat its fruit at random. They were forbidden to cut the ripe tree down and take the ripened fruits as they would from an ordinary banana or plantain tree. The villagers believed that if the deceased spirits were appeased, they would help the family reap bountifully in the new crop year. They were supposed to stop causing mischief and hardship for the surviving members of the family.

This was a practice handed down from past generations. The coming of the West with Christianity has diminished these practices. Individuals still practice some witchcraft and voodoo to a limited degree. The second sacrifice the boy witnessed was more secretive than the first. The boy's own father practiced a form of *"Bosum"*, a fetish worship or belief. The ingredients of the *"Bosum"*, were a very smooth rock, some form of vegetable, and a mound of dried earth the size of a tennis ball. The fetish had three or four white shells placed equidistant and opposite each other on the rounded ball. The last ingredient was the horn of a small bush antelope found in West Africa.

At the time of worship, the worshipper would go into his bedroom alone. He would break a chicken egg on the ingredients. He would rub each with the egg "gelatin" in a distinct fashion and ask for blessings and protection of himself, his family or a mission he was about to embark upon.

His father usually kept his sacrificial dish under his bed. As Christianity engulfed their regions with missionaries, the old man worshipped this *"Bosum"* less and less frequently. The boy believes his father has totally forsaken such practice. In fact when he talks now days, he usually says, "by the grace of God" or "if God is willing", then ends his statement.

Those were the days of savagery, when the heathens raged and the people imagined vain things because they didn't know any better. The boy recognizes that he owes limitless gratitude to all wise God. He purified the barks of young forest trees, which the boy and siblings used to wipe themselves, especially when the ground leaves were too decayed to be used as toilet paper or the leaves on the branches were too high to be reached in those jungles.

The indoctrination of youths is about the same in the various tribal societies. The rites are to teach them early responsibilities - keeping traditions, gender roles, as well as genital circumcision. Health reasons may have something to do with the rites also.

The boy at manhood had a girlfriend. She told him of one of the secrets of the *"Sandee Bush."* The *"Sandee Bush"* is the name of the girls' training camp where girls in the Kpelle tribe went to learn to be a woman. The boy's girlfriend was from the Bassa tribe. She told the boy that the girls are circumcised for two main reasons. First and foremost it was to be able to please their husbands and to facilitate sexual intercourse.

Secondly it was a way to keep themselves clean so fluids wouldn't accumulate in the "inner lips" causing germs to build up, that caused bad odors.

The boy himself did not go to the *"Poro Bush"*, the camp for the boys in the Kpelle tribe. He left the village early to go to the big city, before *Gha-Muu* could kill him. *Gha-Muu* is the name of the male country devil responsible for catching the young men, killing them, and reincarnating them as brand new and better men for the villages in all respect. The passage to manhood or womanhood was very secretive. For the duration that they were gone to the *"Sandee Bush"*, as they are commonly called, the boy never laid his eyes on his two sisters while they tarry forever it seemed. As the drums beat, they danced, and marched away. So did they reappear, shinning, beautiful and grown young ladies that they had become. They no longer insulted the young boys who were trying to "get fresh" with them. They smiled, instead of a wild laughter. They were more tolerant of their siblings than before. They now could comb their own hair, and care for their appearance, without mother telling them to "prepare hot water" for the family to bathe or cook the family meals. In both male and female

"Grebo Bushes", the "Zowe" is in charge of the camp's operation and have the final say so in all matters.

In the tribal society in which the boy was born, it is worthy to note that when a person is born, he or she is given only one name. That child is identified as the son or daughter of the father's first name, an adjective if there is an appropriate one, such as son of short Jimmy.

The second method was to use the father's societal name after applying his first name such as Jimmy Dewa. The big difference here is that no boy or girl, man or woman who had not yet been indoctrinated into the tribal society could call that person son of or daughter of Jimmy Dewa, and not be held in contempt of societal violation. This violation in essence was disrespect to the (Dewa name). Only people older than Jimmy Dewa who had been indoctrinated into the men and women's society could call the Dewa name and not be held in contempt. A mutual settlement in such matter was an apology to Mr. Dewa and a promise not to repeat the offense. It is even of a notoriety that when a boy or girl was indoctrinated into the tribal society, she or he got a second new name that was not of the father's last name. An example would be if a boy named John were indoctrinated. He would come out of the society bush and be called Brown, even though the father's last name was not the same. His birth name John, then would become a societal name. Societal name is a name given after indoctrination into the *"Poro* or *Sandee"* society. Only people who had been indoctrinated could now call him John Brown. All non-indoctrinates could now call him only Brown.

Chapter 31

The Burden and The Glory

Living in the wild the boy watched the woodpeckers hollow out trees. These trees were dead or partially dying from exposure to the elements. They dug the holes for their homes and raised their young in them. The birds of the jungle had no "adverse weather" like the boy and other villagers from which to shelter themselves. Most African birds, as most birds of the tropics, loved rainstorms. They provided their best hunting times. Most bugs, especially flying bugs are blown from their hide-away, usually from beneath leaves into the warring paths of the birds, making their hunt successful.

Living in the West African jungle was like living in a different time zone, as far as weather is concerned. It was very different from northwest Ohio, where dew falls at night, wetting and dampen the grasses, trees, and low leafy shrubs. By early morning, the dew has evaporated due to a bright rising sun. Short showers occur here and there. The afternoon is generally mild, with brisk sunshine off and on, and a sudden cool evening. In the West African jungle big and tall trees blocked the sun, hence dew condensed on the leaves and foliage on the narrow paths to the farms. The misery was multiplied after a rainfall mornings or evenings.

Leaving the village almost every morning to go to the farm was one of the times the tribal children hated. Their bare feet always got wet. Their cold shoulders ached, as did their arms too at times. This was the result of overgrown shrubs and young trees that inhabited the winding, narrow, foot-made paths to the farms. Shrubs whipped and rubbed against their legs and arms. Yearly or every two years when a new "cut and burn farm" was made, they would have to push through the foliage to forge the path.

The boy remembers how he had to carry a heavy *kinjah* on his back. The load of foodstuff was going to the marketplace to be sold for money. The heaviness of this load was due to ignorance on the part of his father. Allowing such a young child to do such manual labor had left a bitter taste in the boy's mouth and mind to this day. A second time the heavy load almost sunk his neck into his feeble body. He believes he was allowed to carry these "too heavy" loads to test his true boyhood, not manhood since he was not yet a man. For the one and a half-hour walk, the boy rested every twenty to thirty minutes. His father later boasted how Lablekgahe carried those heavy loads. The lessons the child learned were two fold. First it taught the child how to do important things for himself and second it taught the child that he had no one but himself to depend on for important projects.

Chapter 32

The One and Only Village Trader

In the quest to satisfy ambition and gain some financial strength, a stranger came into the village borders one day. This Mandingo man knew something about trading that the natives of this village did not know. He hired some men of the town to make a "cut and burn" farm on a parcel of land. Cut and burn farm is one cut with a machete and axe without modern equipment such as a tractor. He paid some women of the village to scratch and plant a large peanut farm. At the time, peanuts were being exported by the 100-pound bag. When the peanuts were harvested and dried, he paid the village children a penny per pound to peel the dry nuts from the shell. Since the children had never worked for money and did not go to school, they stayed up late shelling peanuts. Of course they would become sleepy in the morning on their way to the farms.

After about two years, peanuts became plentiful and were devalued. This trader soon changed strategy and began paying men and boys to climb kola trees to pick the nuts. He began trading in kola nuts. These were more profitable to trade than peanuts. Since neither he nor the natives were educated in modern agricultural planting and mass production, he soon found less and less kola nuts to buy and trade. Besides, many of the natives who farmed for a living began to lapse behind in planting their rice farms. His trading efforts helped educate some of the village natives. They began to find kola nuts and other natural goodies in their environments to sell in the open marketplace or to some storeowners. They realized they no longer needed the trader.

Chapter 33

The Birthday Dilemma of Most Tribal People

The boy's dilemma about his age is still a mystery to him. When he was born, his parents did not know how to read and write. They did not know the importance of birth dates, so they did not keep any birth records, not even stones, shells, or certain seeds to tell the age of their children. When the boy started school, he did not know his birthdate or how old he was. Eventually he asked his parents. They began to count the number of rice farms produced since the boy was born. The problem with this type of record is that some farms took longer to complete than those farms that failed or nearly failed. Lacking accurate information, they tried to link important events within the country or in the world with his birth, but they still could not tell the date, day of the week, or the exact year he was born.

To deal with his dilemma, the boy picked his own birth date and the year he believes he was born. He based these upon world events and his older sister being about two years older than he was. That too he guessed, based on how his parents had other siblings after his birth. He chose December 1948 because his parents told him he was born during the last month of the year and at harvest time for them. They reasoned together it was about three harvest after World War II not counting the harvest of war-ending year.

Chapter 34

Human Sexuality among the Boy's Village

The boy knew nothing about sexuality in his early village life. When he was a child, he saw his sisters and young aunt "pee" often. The urine came from a little pink skin, but was a red color. Red was one of three main colors that all other colors fitted among or in between in that tribal society. The urine came from a little red hole referred to as *wolo-yah*. In Kpelle dialect, that means "water hole". Both little boys and little girls had a water hole.

Little village boys would curse each other by saying *Eh-togo-yah*, meaning "your water hole". Once the boy overheard some teenagers of his village talking. They said if any boy wanted to increase the size and length of his water hole all he had to do was to whip it against a banana tree from side to side. That would cause it to grow bigger and longer. This had to be done twice or more a week. Some of the not-so-handsome boys tried it, and it gave them some recognition by some of the village's bigger girls.

Before all of this, the boy had gotten into trouble with his father for a sexual indiscretion. He was caught behind a mud-dubbed house with a little girl of his same age. They were trying to do "bad thing," slang for having sex. Neither knew what sex was or meant, yet they stood close together trying very hard to get their private parts to touch each other. To them that was having sex. The boy's father spanked him and the little girl's mother took her into the house.

As the boy got a little bigger, he inadvertently spotted the *wolo-yah* of a bigger girl. She was squatting on the playground with her *bumba*, a g-string type cloth panty, not so properly tied. From what he knows now, the girl was reaching the age of puberty. Her pink thing was bigger, more vivid and had scattered short strands of hair forming around it. Before he could get closer to take a second look in awe, the young girl adjusted her legs, covered the view and smiled at the boy. The boy gave her a hard look as if to say, "you will be mine one day when I become a man."

In this particular tribe, and most tribal societies, the young men and women were given in marriage against their will. A young man, Cousin George's older brother, boasted to other young men of the village, that he made out with a particular girl, but he was not going to marry her, no way. The elders of the village frowned upon this act. They believed every young man ought to get married.

The boy's older aunt was made to get engaged to a big man from another village. He was handsome and strong in the eyes of the boy and by most village standards, but his aunt was not interested in him at all. The engagement (which was in essence the young man living with the family for a while until the young lady caught his eye and agreed to be his bride) did not materialize. The young man stayed around for about one farming season and finally moved on in search of a bride.

One young woman of the boy's village was made to marry against her will. Therefore she would let the young man fall asleep at night. While he snored with his mouth open, she would cough up mucus and spit it down his throat. He would roll to his side and swallow it. Whenever she was sick with the cold, he had the cold too. She told this terrible story to her friends and family after the one-year arranged marriage did not work out. Divorce in the tribe was frowned upon by the elders of the village and was not sanctioned at all.

From Jimi's experience, he believes an individual's choice for a life partner should be left to those two to decide for themselves. Society or culture should not interfere in this matter. And God should be the ultimate judge of an individual's choice for a life partner.

PART IV

Jimi Daniel Dillon

Chapter 35

More Education of the Boy

The education of the boy involved many twists, turns, and circumstances, both adverse and beneficial. The boy remembers the singing of such folklore as "Yankee Doodle went to Town riding on a pony, Old froggie went a courting and he did ride uh-huh, uh-huh, and Jack and Jill went up the hill." Those were sung by his first master's grandchildren while bathing and doing short running hops at play.

Their father was an ex-slave's son. The boy thought he had the best and worst of both worlds at times. Here was a tribal servant learning American values. He learned to sing parts of those songs without stopping to think of what they implied or their origin and real meanings.

After the boy came to America, hearing those same songs and learning their original meanings did leave him chuckling at their nostalgic appeal.

The boy's education was also influenced by the coming of the West to the shores of West Africa in modem times. This was after the slave traders came in colonial times and wrought havoc and atrocities among the African tribes and their families. It was after Westerners bought black people as human cargo.

The coming of the West into Africa in modem times was both good and bad, as natives were exposed to new ways of life. Exposing an ignorant person or persons to a new good thing does not necessarily mean that the person will grasp how to benefit from it. An example is the boy's excitement over his first automobile ride to Monrovia. During the three-hour ride, the boy suffered miserably from the diesel fumes and threw up as soon as he stepped off the truck in Monrovia.

The boy had nodded yes every time Cousin George asked him if he was all right, when, in fact, he was not all right. His lack of knowledge about the automobile, its' fuel stench, and the bumpiness of the ride caused him misery. Had Cousin George educated him, the boy may have been better prepared to deal with it. Perhaps he might have psyched himself up to deal with the new situation. The goodness of western education coming to Africa was that it helped open up the continent in many ways. The various opportunities that education makes possible are assets that Africa needed. The same educational system failed to reach the masses or to empower the substandard governments of Africa to educate the masses of their citizens. This coupled with bad Western influences has caused the continent to worsen beyond western-style poverty. Africans could and did manage to survive in cultural poverty unlike beyond the western-style poverty.

Unlike Santa Claus in western cultures, who brings gifts to the deserving loved ones, poor boys children of the West African natives in the city, dressed like Santa Claus and danced for pocket change, from door to door in their neighborhoods. They made their own music and beat that does not sound like or resemble anything like "Jingle Bells." One such song went like this:

Soldier, Soldier, Soldier

Clique-ma-ta ley take (claim mortality-means solders do take life (kill). There was a lead singer and the rest in the group responded as back-up singers. As the songs echoed, the dancer captivated his audience, jumping, twisting, and turning - coming down on split legs in a break dance style. The song was adapted from *"Soldier, Soldier, Soldier, Will You Marry Me?"*

By the way, the boy believes that break dance was copied from one of their performances. Perhaps photographed? Or recorded on paper (idea), the boy does not know. But he can show you how it was done before "Break Dance" came into being and moved in America and the western world.

Some of the children of this West African city of Monrovia, also used another *"Beggar Dancer"* called the *"Old Man Beggar."* He, too, was like the Santa Clause that danced for money at Christmas time. He and his singing entourage went from house to house begging for money. While they sang, *"Old Man Beggar, John the Beggar,"* repeatedly, he, too, danced (surreptitiously). Randomly, to the live lipsy and makeshift instrumental music. You talk about "Santa" bringing you presents at Christmas time, but in this part of the world, some of the children, especially the aborigines, became their own Santas, singing, dancing and begging for pocket change at Christmas time to buy little goodies to eat, or go to the movies.

Oh, yes, by the way, this "Old Man Beggar" was usually dressed to resemble the "famous Santa" known around the western and perhaps the eastern world— the perception is that, he did not usually have a red velvety suit to dress in while doing his begging dance. Rather, he wore a homemade outfit of old rags or one stitched together of various pieces of cloth by a local tailor. Daniel and other servants also danced to the tune of their masters, or we were out, out as said in "Baseball."

America introduced Western culture to the coast of West Africa, but stop short of making that most sought after culture a reality for the majority of the African. Indeed, had America in her wisdom, and she is wise…assisted the little west African country with higher education, and technology, the boy and the majority of his countrymen would have realized the true taste and value of Western culture and civilization to its fullest, within their own borders.

The millions of dollars of assistance and loans America gave Liberia went into the pockets of the very few Americo-Liberians. The boy considers himself a member of the working class, with average income and lifestyle. Very few Africans can earn a decent living in that part of Africa. Except for those that worked in the government. That was before the Civil War broke out in "Evil April of 1982." A Master Sergeant seized power from the Americo-Liberians, but made matters worse because he was uneducated and not prepared as a leader. He took the country from bad to worse both politically and economically.

The boy is saying that when the west came on the shores of West Africa to trade in modern times, they should have educated the natives. An education which would have equipped them to fend for themselves "how to get those good things that the west (America) introduced them to." Take for example, the Firestone Plantation and Rubber Company. She operated in Liberia on a contracted 100,000 acres of land, planting and taking rubber out of Liberia. This contract was made with the Liberian government for approximately 99 years.

Take BF Goodrich Tires and Rubber Company also. She operated in Liberia for a very long time, doing the same damn thing. Also the LAMCO Joint-Venture Mining Company, who took iron ores out of Liberia for a very long time. It was good that these companies came to help the poor natives make a living? Paying them fifteen cents to forty cents an hour, maximum. "Bad", in that they have failed to establish manufacturing plants in the country and educating the local employees with real skills and real jobs of (how to make tires and a steel factory). When they pulled out of the country, for one reason or another, after making their millions to billions of dollars, those companies closed their doors. Leaving the local employees without another means of making a living. Had factories been built, perhaps another buyer or a local entrepreneur would have taken over and continued their operations.

This seems to be another exploitation of the West African "people of color." The West African natives had now tasted a good thing, but the good things ended abruptly. They had lost their basic skills of jungle survival. Many "hung around" after plantation closures. They are still hoping that the west (America) will return and bring back some more good things. Many of the educated left and are now in America.

Another *"evil"* of the west (America) is that some of the goods that they brought to the shores of the West African were not all good. They "west" failed to teach the natives of the harmful side effects of some of those goods. The failure to educate the natives of the dangers of using chemical agents, such as soap, is a good example. A particular soap, commonly referred to as the "Firestone" (blue) soap was used in the creeks, lakes and rivers to wash clothes and take baths. That soap and others killed off basic food chains in the creeks, lakes and rivers. The small fresh water mussels, oysters, crabs, crawfish, fish in general, died out as a result. This unintentional killing of food supplements in the various towns and villages depleted their (natives') first source of protein gathering place. Those that live along the coast of large bodies of water even used dynamite to blow schools of fish, destroying the ecosystem of that body of water. The American electrical company "**SHEMAG**" (Salala Hydro Electric Management Group) was responsible for the dynamite. Those that live further in the jungle areas could only "trap" so much, and so long, before killing off a certain species of game. Since they no longer could find anything in the waters they fished before. Remember that the west brought the guns, too.

That lack of education the West failed to give the natives has also caught up with the West itself, especially the Americans. We (Africans) needed "Green Peace," then, and we do need them now! For America's failure to educate home and abroad, just look at her coast, her great rivers, lakes and common shorelines. For there you will find discarded chemicals, empty bottles, cans, plastic goods, containers and tar containing materials, etc. Some are even floating in the waterways. The boy as a poet writes,

> *The "west" took her natural resources*
> *The "east" —her cash*
> *Leaving Liberia awashed*
> *in poverty!*

*The Lebanese Traders, etc.

Chapter 36

The "Doe" Factor

The atrocities allowed by the West, especially America, as the mother country of Liberia were by no means an accident. America was well aware of the potential for civil war and violence to happen in a distant small country on the West African coast. America had supported the country's autocratic government for years, especially under the leadership of William Tubman. After his twenty-seven years of leadership, the country crashed, even as he, through death passed the torch to his vice president Tolbert. Yes, the Big T&T, the Liberian government, allowed only a one-party system, which the United States supported with millions of dollars over several decades. Liberia was founded by the American colonization society between the years 1820-1822.

When the U.S. interest was diminishing through several factors, she allowed the demon of war to rain "hell" on this poor little country. Who do you think made and supported the "Samuel Doe," the "Prince Johnson," and their kind? If the United States had acted with the same concern and quickness as she did with the little island country of Grenada, all that bloodshed, carnage, and extreme poverty caused by those armed "killer Marauders" would have been averted. Marauders were self-made soldiers or anybody who could get a gun calling themselves factions.

Liberia, which had never had an aborigine as president, lost her only chance in this century, when Samuel K. Doe became greedier, disheartened and a ruthless killer over night, as a Liberian "self-made" president. His cowardly and illiterate style of leadership soon made him a more brutal autocrat than Tubman or any other predecessor. Samuel Doe was an Army Master Sergeant who seized power from then President William R. Tolbert, Jr., in Liberia. He killed the president, his thirteen or more cabinet ministers and made himself president. He died by the guns at the end of his ten year terror and reign. Prince Johnson, a member of Charles Taylor's rebel group helped to launch a successful offensive against the corrupt Doe government in the capital city of Monrovia.

This happened after Taylor and Johnson broke ranks due to differences in handling their fighting men. Prince Johnson then became a separate rebel group leader like Charles Taylor. Both began fighting each other's forces, at the same time trying to oust Doe's ill prepared forces or the fraction of what he had left in the executive mansion. Prince Johnson and his men were successful in toppling Doe and his men later.

The first rebel group leader, Charles Taylor, who challenged Doe and Doe was later killed by Prince Johnson, did win the 1997 general presidential elections by attrition. Taylor, attuning himself with most of the illiterate natives who live in the countryside, made his name familiar to them—positively or negatively. Therefore, when election time came, the majority of the native and illiterate people could identify his name and voted for him. Whatever Taylor did during those rebel escapades (armed men roaming the countryside), some good and some bad, made him popular among the candidates running for president.

The boy recently read an article in an African newspaper, printed in Houston, Texas. The article spoke of "African Democracy" being practiced by the military leader of Nigeria, Strongman Abacha, when he was alive. The writer also advise, the West especially the United States, to let such political system be practiced in Africa, especially to let Abacha continue to lead his people in Nigeria.

But the boy has a problem with such a vision. We all must remember that a democracy is a government of the people, for the people, and by the people. When one seizes powers, makes himself/herself a leader of a country, and cancels the election process, jailing the predominant winner of that election process, we no longer have a democratic government but a "demon-cratic government." One has only to look back at the long history of Africa and her practice of African Democracy and it is easy to see what chaos it has left the continent in, carnage, mayhem, marauders, extreme poverty, chaos and most of all, hopelessness.

Yes, most Africans have lost hope in their own land and leaders of their nativity. Should Africa continue to practice "African Democracy?" The boy thinks not. Instead, let Africa try a little bit of "Western Democracy" and by God, he thinks she'll love it.

Chapter 37

Touching on the Classes of People in Liberia

In Liberia there were two social and economic classes, the "have's" and the "have-none". The boy doesn't believe there were any rich people when the Mayflower landed in 1822. A group of ex-slaves and sons of ex-slaves settled in Liberia, but not without a fight.

The boy remembers several history pamphlets in early elementary school from which told of several tribal wars with the new settlers, the colonists. He recalls that one famous "heroine" of one of those was called Matilda Newport. Even today a Liberian street is named in her honor. In every fight in which blood is shed, the victor usually lose some blood too, even if it is just a bleeding scratch. Perhaps it could be a relative who was distantly involved, or the victor could be hurt inwardly, such as wounded pride or character destruction, or the wounded may be conscious. Taking another human's life is still one of the worst crimes in God's book, and the worst in all human societies of past and present.

According to this homemade history pamphlet, after a long and bitter insurrection between tribal warriors and the colonists (ex-slaves), the colonist fighters became wounded, wearied, and hungry. They had no time for growing gardens and small farms due to the wars. On one such evening, after a long day of fighting with the native warriors, the colonists' camp was fast asleep. Even the watchman fell asleep. As fate would have it, Matilda Newport, an older member of the group, woke up with the strong urge to smoke her old homemade pipe. As she prepared the homegrown dried tobacco, she picked up a red-hot coal from the hearth of the fireplace to put it into her pipe.

When she lifted up her head, she saw the tribal warriors stealthily advancing on the colonists' camp. The tribesmen had their bows with arrows drawn, machetes drawn, and were swinging wooden clubs. With no time to wake the camp for self-defense, she immediately took the coal out of her pipe and placed it into the "standing and aimed cannon" that was to be used in the event of an attack by the tribesmen.

Since the cannon was already prepared with no adjustment needed or necessary, the gunpowder ignited quickly. The big gun killed more than half of the advancing tribal warriors. The rest ran wild into the bushes leaving behind their wounded and their homemade weapons. The shock of a gun so big, so loud, and so deadly caused the many tribal groups never to unite again to try an attack on the colonists. After that last battle, the colonist enjoyed a newfound peace. They no longer had former slave masters watching them; they no longer had tribal war parties trying to attack them. The colonists prospered slowly, but surely. So much did they enjoy total control of this newfound Liberia, that in 1847 Liberia became the first black independent country on the continent of Africa.

With American and other humanitarian organizations supporting the new Liberia, she would be ruled by sons of ex-slaves, commonly called Americo-Liberians, until the evil April of 1982 to 1996. And in view of the leadership of this little West African country, the boy writes a poem:

<u>Liberia</u>

I tell you a tale of a state—Liberia
'Twas so poor
Yet mineral rich…
Of fine natural resources, she was!

Of one the West* wouldn't risk.

At least to Soviets' visitation - habitation

Until the Cold War ended.
Now the illiterate few
Felled the mass erudite of power abuse
In evil April of '82 to '96

Now they so poor**,
Politically, socially and economically.
USA
Very poor

And in support of his poem, the boy remembers a closed door discussion by some college and senior high school students. They said that the late and former president of Ghana, Dr. Kwame Nkrumah, had visited Red China. Upon his return, he addressed the O.A.U. (Organization of African Unity) and challenged them not to let Western "carbon copy" democracy continue to diminish the political, social, and economic power of Africa. He called Africa to unite as individual states to amass its powers for a new direction into the future, a new diversion of its resources to member's states, and for Africa to wean itself from that of total Western influence and foreign aid. Unfortunately Dr. Nkrumah was over-thrown by members of his own government in the military in 1966. He died in exile in Romania in 1972.

It was rumored that a mole within his one party, a "democratic government," had led the overthrow. Most African leaders feared this noble, yet radical idea of Dr. Kwame Nkrumah noble in that it would change the economic face of Africa forever before the outside world, yet radical in that it might bring Communism to the African continent.

Another ingredient that seasoned the fears of some members of the O.A.U. was that they thought Dr. Nkrumah would become president for life over the other African leaders. They also feared that their individual powers over their people in their individual countries would be diminished to that of governorship.

But the boy knows better, that their greatest fear was losing all the economic packages they received over the years in the name of "development" for their individual countries. These monies ended up in their pockets, foreign schools for their children, their family businesses, and finally their Swiss bank accounts.

In the early 70's, the late and former president of Liberia, William V. S. Tubman, died in office. World newspapers and reports put his cash assets at over $4 million in Swiss bank accounts. With his meager salary as president of this small and poor West African country, there is no way he could have amassed such a savings during his twenty-five plus years as president of Liberia. Tubman is credited as being the best president Liberia ever had. He was considered one of the greatest leaders of modem-day Africa. But Tubman had a big flaw, and the boy knows that you know what it was.

Unlike Gandhi of India, Tubman allowed for the exploitation of the native villagers by foreigners, especially Lebanese, Syrians, Indians, and other smaller groups. Due to his "open door policy," any foreign investor could and did come into the country, make money, and take all out to home banks as well as foreign banks. None of these "foreign investors" cared to educate the citizens in their trade, but took the citizens' monies, and left them poor and ignorant. In fact, most of the employees in the stores and restaurants were the illiterate ones. This was done purposely so that the employer's trade secrets could not be learned by indigenous citizens. There were very few employed during Tubman's latter years in office. The boy noticed that most stores had a husband and wife team, a brother or brother-in-law or a grown son, besides the one Liberian "helping hand."

Tubman was also unlike Dr. Martin Luther King, Jr. King submitted his body to jail beatings, beatings, etc. in his attempt to try to end racial segregation and bring about equality for all people in America. He sacrificed his life for those causes. Tubman, on the other hand, with his one-party "democratic" goverrunent was actually an old autocracy. It later became modem totalitarianism.

Tubman jailed many people who dared speak against his government. He would later soften his heart and take the "trouble-maker" out of jail without a trial. He would "pat the person on the back," give him a promotion in his regular government job or create a job for him. It was a "keep your mouth closed and let me do my thing" arrangement. The boy learned from a second hand source that a son of a well-respected government official had come from abroad (U.S. or England). He had gone to the University of Liberia and began to express his political views of how things "ought to be run at the university, in the Liberian government, etc." What soon followed was an admonishment of his parents for his acts. It is said that Tubman made money available and a one-way ticket for the young man to take his radical ideas back to where he came from and continue his schooling there.

The children of the West have plenty of time for school and play. The youthful native servants did not. They worked for their masters/guardians with very little time to play, if any. On weekends they usually hand washed clothes on washboards. Even at the age of puberty, they worked with very little or no contact with peers, except at school. And that contact was brief. Most servants went to afternoon, evening, or night school. Night school was usually for the adults.

Once a child was in the servant "role," he/she had to remain there to be able to make contacts for jobs after graduation from high school. The master-guardian usually recommended a servant who "hung in there" to the end. If a servant defected or quit a master-guardian, he/she lost all chances of contacts and no one was willing to give him/her a job without a letter of recommendation from a master-guardian. Since no one knew his original native parents, he was almost certainly doomed to fail in Liberian society. The boy's fellow servant, Lafayette, is a classic example. He quit his master-guardian and did not go to school. Lafayette became a "here now boy." "Here now boys" were mostly young men who sold pieces of clothing and other odds and ends to households on street corners or door to door.

The ruling class of Liberians, were very conscious of their superiority over the uneducated natives. They would intimidate people of seemingly lower status with the phrase, "Do you know who I am", or "Don't you know who I am?" This was done usually to demand respect instantly. Even if that individual was wrong, he tried to turn the odds in his favor with that infamous phrase. Some would ask, "Who are you? I mean, your father's name?" The second question was usually when one went out to find a job at a governmental agency or office.

So, it was mandatory for most servants to persevere if they hoped to have a decent future. Daniel was blessed. He had a female friend in the eleventh and twelfth grades. They both graduated together. He was the sweetheart of this girl's friend. The friend had a married friend who worked at the refinery. She sent the boy to this male friend with a letter to help him find a job. The male friend in turn made Daniel the "go for" for their love affair. He, in turn, helped the boy get hired at the refinery.

Groups of the jungle-dwelling natives did decide to move in masses to the city of Monrovia, Liberia's capital, but the boy does not know exactly when the migration started, perhaps the mid-'60s. But when they arrived, they ended up renting the basements, oh excuse me, the bottom of "foundations" of some of the Americo-Liberians houses. Based on their educational "status quo" and belief, they were better than the Liberian natives, the city dwellers would not allow the natives to live in adjacent rooms. The Americo-Liberians felt that they must at all times be above the natives.

Some of the Americo-Liberians, after building a better house than the zinc old-frame houses left to them by their forefathers, ended up renting rooms to the aborigines, and their grown children with or without families. The rental income added "better living" conditions to their Americo-Liberian families. This living arrangement added to the already low status of the natives—already on the lowest end of the Liberian economic totem pole.

The boy believes that all this happened after the natives had tasted the "Western venison's" (easy and good living in the city or so it may have seemed to the unsuspecting natives at the time). The coastal natives were already living in make shift, rusted, crusty zinc houses. Those living arrangements and conditions affecting the natives further divided and alienated the "have's" and the "have none."

Some of the Liberian ruling class members so despised the native citizens that they sometimes took advantage of them. Unless gross negligence could be shown on the part of the ruling class official, he or she could and did get away with murder - literally. Even when negligence was shown against one such Americo-Liberian, he was let go free after he ran over and killed an aborigine pedestrian. The official was driving recklessly, but the police charged the dead man with jaywalking. The boy believes the ruling class man who committed the killing was once police chief of Liberia.

The boy himself was involved in a similar situation of, but there was no death involved. While he worked at a gas station, the driver of a bank's president ran over his left foot, intentionally. The driver was coming to get his weekly fill-up. He blew the "Benz horn" for the boy to move out of his way. The boy was busy pumping gas for another customer. In his hateful hurry and pride that he was driving a Mercedes Benz, and for a bank's president, he just could not wait! He drove on top of the boy's foot. When the boy cried and complained of the injury, he replied, "If this big car had passed over your foot, it would be broken." The man refused to apologize to the boy. He got his gas from the other attendant, A.S. Kothe, who tried to get him to tell the boy that he was sorry, but he still refused to admit to his crime and to apologize.

About six months later, the same Benz he used to flatten the boy's left foot - flattened his body on the only Liberian highway. The boy did not know about this until he asked his friend Kothe why the driver did not buy their gas anymore. He replied, "Oh, did you not hear? That guy who ran over your foot last summer, his Benz crashed and flattened his body. People think he may have been speeding too fast or sleeping at the wheel," he explained. The boy instantly looked up and stated, "There is a higher justice, I tell you, Kothe." And he rejoiced that he himself did not render the vengeance, but his maker did. (Hebrews 10:30)

This "heathen child," as he was commonly called by his masters, had found God, thanks to Jesus Christ, who saved his soul in the summer of 1965. He was heavily involved in the church and work of Christ at the time of his mistreatment by the Benz driver. The church held prayer meetings almost every weekend at somebody's house in the city. This type of service moved from neighborhood to neighborhood. They were so strong in the Lord that his last master-guardian named the group "The Evening Prayer and Deliverance Band." People came from far and near, one such confessing his sins of using human parts in "voodoo" to get a high position in the then Liberian government. He got the job, went overseas, and served his country, but later his health started failing him and his sins started haunting him. His confessions led to special prayer, fastening, and tarry for him. His sins were forgiven and his health restored, but he lost his family "overseas" during this terrible pursuit.

The little prayer band eventually became a small church. Today that church is also a small elementary school serving the community. The school was named after the then president of Liberia. It's called the William V. S. Tubman Silver Jubilee School. It was founded by the boy's last master-guardian. The boy himself taught at the little school while he was in high school.

Manuel Noriega sits in jail to "rot" for political corruption, killings, and drug trafficking to America. Castro of Cuba was ostracized to his native Cuba, punished economically for exercising his right to introduce Communism to his country. Now, the African dictators—excluding Nelson Mandela of South

Africa, are responsible for gross genocide within their countries. Those same leaders, or most of them, are being prepared by the West to be "fattened up" for their crimes against humanity. I would hope that Christ should come and render true justice, for there is no justice anywhere. By the way, by whose invention did these evils of the dictators come? By the West of course—with its big bad guns did these black dictators almost annihilate their kinfolk, unlike the season of the Cold War when the West shut its eyes while African dictators filled their pockets and ran to the Swiss and U.S. banks. Every third world African leader that has left office by an over-throw or natural death has been proven to be a millionaire, with funds in foreign banks, not even taking into consideration their home based assets.

The West must make an about-face. Since President Clinton has shown his face in Africa, America and other allies must monitor their assistance packages and every penny spent in Africa in the name of "development." Otherwise monies spent in the name of "development" will all end up in their pockets and their overseas bank accounts when the development fails to occur.

Chapter 38

Liberianism - Non-Cohesive in Cultural Bonding

The boy "no sabeen" in the sciences of anthropology, sociology, or even human psychology, but the boy has a problem with all Liberians, especially Liberian-Americans. The question he asks is, "why do other nationalities work together, get along so well but not Liberians or Liberian-Americans in general?" And he is not talking about relatives either. The boy cites many examples. He was a vice president for the Liberian Associations of N.W. Ohio, Toledo Chapter. In that organization and others statewide, there were always confusion, nepotism, and favoritism. Even in Houston, where Jimi now lives, there was a big and growing Liberian Association, but it soon died down because people wanted things to go their way or no other way. A disgruntled member even took a gun to one of the gatherings. That was how he planned to make his point or to make himself heard.

On the other hand, the boy sees other nationalities prospering and holding together. Nigerians have a high percentage of professionals throughout the United States. They have several individual and group businesses as well. The Asians have bought out half or more of southwest Houston. The Indians, and the Ghanians, also work together. So, then, why not Liberians or Liberian-Americans? Liberians and Liberian-Americans would rather sit and gossip about one another than lend a hand to a less fortunate member of that society or a neighbor. Some would backbite and put down others just because they may be ahead in the game of life. That is, being fortunate to have a good job might cause that individual to alienate him from the others.

The boy can only speculate that the master-servant relationship is the main culprit. Some of the masters' children still regard themselves as better than the sons of the aborigines. And some of the sons of the aborigines despise the children of the past masters who dominated the aborigines' lives for so long - politically, economically, and socially. In general, the lack of an early opportunity to develop the young aborigines' minds could be a reason why the sons of aborigines despise the sons of Americo-Liberians. Another disadvantage for the boy was being bom in the wrong place—the African jungle. The master-servant relationship also prohibited him from prospering as the early necessary and basic education that all young minds need to be molded with, was denied him. It is very hard for a child denied this early educational molding, to recover. And it is hard for that child to be able to compete on an international or global level—as other citizens of the Western world have succeeded in doing.

Let us now come together as one people with one reason, "brotherly tolerance," and understanding. If we put our individual differences aside, we can work together as a team, and for the common good of all concerned, even our nationalism. Perhaps our coming together, if we would, will appease America and the rest of the world to help us, help our brothers and sisters in the war-torn land of ours—Liberia! The once "sweet land of liberty."

Now that President Clinton has visited Africa, the boy hopes that the West in general will not treat Africa like the "slip-slide" servant. He was one whose master used him in two distinct roles. At nighttime, he was made the masters' "honey." But in the daytime, she referred to him as *"Ro-gues,"* or "Ruckus." The servant is described as "slip slide" because he did not know what to make of himself. He did not know whether to consider himself as an elite (as the master and her children) or just a plain old servant.

In consideration of this servant's dilemma, a musical artist of Africa (he could well have been a servant himself), wrote and sang the song titled, "Rogues Ruckus." The song goes like this:

> Rogues (Ruckus), don't call me Ruckus.
> In the daytime, you call Ruckus.
> But in the nighttime, you call me honey! etc.
> So, my dear West, you came to Liberia and took our golds, diamonds, ores and rubber! Come now again—with the proper education and training. Bring the Resources—your great economic machines that have made every great nation successful.
> America still does have one of her great satellite stations in Liberia, That she watches all of Africa with.
> America come back and let's start all over our new love relationship.
> We* need you.

On a 1988 visit to Liberia, a billboard caught the boy's eye. "Daffy Duck" advertised "Fanta drink" on the outskirts of the West African city of Monrovia, yet the majority of its populace have not seen Daffy Duck in actuality the cartoon or actors. The boy wondered aloud, "Perhaps Coca-Cola, who makes Fanta drinks, could surprise those poor children and their parents (drinkers of Fanta) with a surprise party one day." The main guest of attraction of course would be Daffy Duck and other cartoon characters. They have often appeared on billboards elsewhere in those parts of the Third World countries to advertise similar products of the Coca-Cola Company. Those children who have wondered who Daffy Duck is, do not have, or have not had, a television set to see Daffy and comrades on it. Bravo, Coca-Cola! Won't you surprise them? The boy has now challenged you!

Chapter 39

Deeds of the Boy

While on the jungle farm as a little child, the boy committed his first heroic deed - at least in the eyes of his late Grandma Lahynahn (pronounced Law-Young). She was affectionately called "Nana" by all her grandkids and others.

It happened late one sultry evening, while Grandma prepared rice to take home for the evening meal. A ricebird flew in and sat right before the little boy's eyes as if to say, "you ain't nothin' and you can't do me any harm." As the bird waited momentarily to swoop down on the rice, which was on a mat drying in the sun, the little boy picked up a piece of dried branch and threw it at the bird sitting on a cassava tree limb. The branch found its mark, and the bird came tumbling down to the ground, like London Bridge. The boy quickly sprang on the frightened and disoriented bird like a cheetah on a rabbit. He ran to his grandma, whose back was turned fanning the chaff off the mortar and pencil-crushed rice. Her eyes bulged with excitement. She remarked, "Whoa! My grandson already a hunter!" When the others came from their daily chores around the farm and bushes, she told them what the boy had done to the pesky ricebird. They all congratulated the little boy for his first act of a successful hunter that he would become some day.

As a young teenager, the boy rescued a drowning youth from the Atlantic Ocean's beach in Monrovia. He had no experience in swimming, but he saw the need and something in him moved him to risk his life and dive into the sweeping wave to pull that little boy out of the ocean. He guessed it was God's will that he help him.

When the boy was in junior high school, he acted again as a hero. A big Muslim family rented or leased a modern concrete house from the boy's last master-guardian. The house was about 500 yards from the all-zinc house in which the boy and the family lived. This was the same house that the boy had helped build.

Across from the rented house a patch of wild weeds had grown over an old 50-gallon barrel. The weeds had choked the barrel so that it was almost hidden from the eye. In the rear of this metal barrel which had probably been used for oil, some Africanized honeybees had built a hive. The boy and others were outside playing with a soccer ball. One of the wives of the renter (he had several) came out of the house, and went into that weeded area looking for twigs to kindle her fireplace, an outdoor open hearth. As she tried to pull a dry piece of stick and some twigs from under the old barrel, she unsuspectingly disturbed the beehive. Immediately the Africanized bees attacked. She screamed to the top of her voice, stunned by the stinging bees. She froze and could not move.

The boy realized that the woman was in deep trouble. He quickly ran to her rescue. He pulled off her top "wrap-around cloth" (they wore more than one). He covered her bee-infested head and hair, picked her up as if she were a small log and ran into their house. He shouted for the door to be closed, for the bees were in pursuit of their prey. The door was slammed. He rubbed the woman's head with the *"lappa"* (wrap-around cloth) to kill the bees that had infested her hair. He killed most of the bees that had followed into the house. People standing around got stung or were chased into hiding. The boy himself was stung several times all over. After the melee, he kept pulling bee stings out of his skin and hair for about two days. He became feverish for about five days.

The lady who was attacked became very sick and took some herbal treatment to alleviate some of her pain. Her husband sent for the boy, when he got home. He thanked the boy for saving his wife's life and gave the boy five U.S. dollars. Yes, a big green U.S. five dollar bill!

The boy's fourth "deed", so to speak, was one done out of necessity. It was a matter of self-preservation. His life was being threatened and, in desperation to save his life, he acted rashly, quickly, yet successfully and probably also prevented a financial loss to his employer. It involved his foiling an attempted robbery at a gas station where the boy worked, August 23, 1975.

The fifth incident that could be considered a good "deed" was not really a deed, but rather an act of civic duty. The boy and friend witnessed a crime being committed against the city of Toledo, Ohio, where he lived. They witnessed park benches being stolen and put in the back of a pickup truck. Being a taxpayer, he thought it was wrong. On his way to report the crime to the police station, he and his friend were further violated. The criminals followed them. Racial slurs were yelled at them, and his automobile windshield was smashed in, and the car was scratched. The boy now considers this incident May 23, 1983 his "Jasper, Texas" experience.

Why? The perpetrators of those crimes against the boy and his friend and the city of Toledo, itself were never punished. They were white. Despite the fact that the police had an address on the criminals, they were never brought to justice as far as the boy knows. The warrant, which was issued for the car owner's arrest, after several refusals to appear in court, is probably in a dead file; if not, expunged. In such matters involving races, the police and city leaders should do more than just daily routine chores. The two police reports that follow tell more about his incident.

CRIME REPORT

POLICE DIVISION
TOLEDO, OHIO
Form 38.1 Rev. 8/81

JUVENILE ☐

1 VICTIM Last, First, Middle (Firm Name, If Business, STATE OF OHIO

DIAL
Warrant
Bar

3 TYPE OF CRIME THEFT

4 Location of Occurrence 7. BROADWAY

6 UCR Code and Number 06-071

7 Type of Premises or Name of Business Where Offense Was Committed WALBRIDGE PARK

8 Bea:

9 Date and Time Occurred 5-23-83 2030

10 Day of Week MON

11 Date and Time Reported 5-23-83 2/20

ROUTING
AIN.
sections
mal Aff.
Of Chief
MIN. SER.
ne Preven.
nm. Rel.
ning
sonnel
EST. SER.
mes/Person
mes/Prop.
uth Ser.
e/Narcotic
LD OPER.
rol
ffic
PP. SER.
mmun.
p. Mgt.
HER
e
w

12 Reporting Person's Name (Last, First, Middle) DILLON, JIMI D

13 Victim's Race | Sex | Age | D.O.B. | Occupation

14 Reporting Person's Residence Address 132 FACE

15 Res Phone 255-0609

16 Victim's Residence Address | City

17 Res Phone

18 Reporting Person's Business Address 1897 W. ALEXIS

19 Bus. Phone 474-5265

20 Victim's Business Address | City

21 Bus Phone

22 WITNESS NO. 1 - NAME (Last, First, Middle) NESBITT ROSIE M

Age 22 | Residence Address 1113 CAMPBELL | City TOL | Res. Phone 244-6867 | Bus Phone

WITNESS NO. 2 - NAME (Last, First, Middle) | Age | Residence Address | City | Res. Phone | Bus Phone

23 VEHICLE Color REL/WHT Year Make Model PICK-UP Style License No. (State, Year) N8LG14 V.I.N. Towed Where?

Registered Owner's Name | Registered Owner's Residence Address
☐ HOLDER
☐ Suspect's ☐ Victim's

24 SUSPECT NO. 1 - NAME (Last, First, Middle) | 25 Race W | 26 Sex M | 27 Age 25-30 | 28 D.O.B | 29 Hgt | 30 Weight | 31 Hair | 32 Eyes

33 Address (Apt. No.) Phone City | 34 Date and Time of Arrest | 35 Advised of Rights? Yes ___ No ___

36 Clothing and Other Identifiers | 37 B.I.R. No. | 38 Arrest Number:

SUSPECT NO. 2 - NAME (Last, First, Middle) | 25 Race | 26 Sex | 27 Age | 28 D.O.B | 29 Hgt | 30 Weight | 31 Hair | 32 Eyes

Records Section No. 333211

ADDRESS (Apt. No.) Phone City | 34 Date and Time of Arrest | 35 Advised of Rights? Yes ___ No ___

Clothing and Other Identifiers | 37 B.I.R. No. | 38 Arrest Number

CRIMES AGAINST PROPERTY - Point Where Entrance Was Made
☐ Force ☒ No Force ☐ Attempt

40 Exact Location of Property When Stolen INSIDE OF WALBRIDGE PARK

Instrument Used (Describe)

42 Method Used To Gain Entrance OPEN PARK

Where Was Occupant At Time of Entrance

44 Trademark of Suspect(s) - Action or Conversation

CRIMES AGAINST PERSON - Weapon, Force, or Means Used
☐ Weapon ☐ Strongarm (No Weapon)

46 Exact Location of Victim at Time of Offense

7 Victim's Activity at Time of Offense

48 Apparent Motive - Type of Property Taken or Obtained

EXACT Words Used By Suspect(s)

0 TYPE OF NARCOTIC:
① Cocaine, Opium | Heroin, Morphine, Marijuana, ② Hashish | ③ Synthetic Narcotics | ④ LSD, PCP, Benzedrine | ⑤ Inhalents | ⑥ Possession of Implements | ⑦ Forging of Prescriptions

51 Dictated for Transcription? Yes ☐ No ☐
52 Follow-up Required? Yes ☒ No ☐

3 TYPE OF GAMBLING:
① Bookmaking (Horses, Sports) | ② Numbers, Lottery | ③ Cards, Dice, Pool, All Others | ④ Bingo

54 ARREST ON:
☐ Warrant ☐ Attachment ☐ View

5 WEAPON Describe Weapon
① Gun ② Knife ③ Hands/Feet ④ Other

56 INDICATE:
① Yard Search ⑦ Detective Notified
② Field Search ⑧ Detective on Scene
③ Area Search
④ Cursory TAB N.C.
⑤ Intensive
⑥ Summons Who Notified/At Scene?

7 PREMISES TYPE
1 Residence
2 Apt/Duplex
3 Hotel/Motel
4 School
5 Church
6 Bar/Restaurant
7 Bank

8 Medical
9 Office Bldg.
10 Manufacturer
11 Gas Station
12 Chain Store
13 Small Business
14 Highway/Street

POINT OF ENTRY & LOCATION
20 Door
21 Window
22 Garage Door
23 Adjacent Premises
24 Other
(Describe Other) CITY PARK

METHOD USED
25 Front 40 Open/Unlocked
26 Rear 41 Body Force
27 Side 42 Pry/Cutting
28 Roof 43 Channel Locks
29 Other 44 Break Glass

58 Street Index | Property | M.O. | Index | Tab

9 Report Made By SHEILA JOHNSON

Officer(s) Name(s) - I.D. No - Unit No 544 LEC.

60 Officer Assigned to Case

61 Supervisor's Approval

2 DISPOSITION 200
① UNFOUNDED ② CLEARED-NO ARREST ③ CLEARED BY ARREST ④ ADJUSTED ⑤ INVESTIGATION CONTINUES ⑥ INACTIVE CASE

54	Quantity	PROPERTY ☒ TAKEN · ☐ RECOVERED (List) Name, Brand, Model, Color, Size, Type, License Number	Serial Number	Value
	1.	BENCH THAT WAS IN PARK BELONGING TO CITY		
		PROP STOLEN		
			Total Value Loss $	

55 EVIDENCE. Where Found, By Whom, Disposition

Evidence Preserved At Scene
a ☐ Possible Fingerprints c ☐ Body Fluids
c ☐ Footprints d ☐ Tool Marks

Disposition of Evidence Removed From Scene (Marked & Tagged)
e ☐ Booked/Property Room g ☐ Investigative Safe
f ☐ Night Property Room h ☐ District Station Property
☐ Flammable ☐ Stor Cab   Property Number

56 DETAILS. (Address the categories listed below, where applicable, in the order they appear.)
(1) List additional victims. (2) List additional witnesses. (3) List additional suspects, descriptions, arrestees, charges.
(4) If juvenile involved as victim or suspect, list parents' names (last, first, middle), phone number, school attended, and whether parents notified.
(5) If victim injured, describe injuries and where treated.
(6) Indicate time and location where victims and witnesses may be contacted later for follow-up.
(7) Indicate if victim, reporting person, witness or suspect gave statement. Record statement on Supplemental Report, if necessary.
(8) Itemize additional property taken, giving name, brand, model, serial no., caliber of guns, identifying marks, and value of each item.
(9) List additional physical evidence, where found, by whom, disposition, and identifying marks.
(10) Provide additional description on vehicle (unusual paint, body, marks, or damage). Describe additional vehicles.
(11) If vehicle stolen, give Title number and value. Car unlocked, keys in ignition? List name of insurance and/or finance company.
(12) Reconstruct the incident - include all necessary elements of the crime.

12) PERSON REPORTING AND WITNESS OBSERVERD THE PASSENGERS FROM # THE ABOVE DESC. VEH. GET OUT AND PICK UP BENCH AND PUT IT INTO THE BACK OF THE ABOVE DESCRIBED VEH. AND DRIVE OFF. HOWEVER THE SUSPECT'S ALSO SAW THE PERSON REPORTING AND THE WITNESS WATCHING AND FOLLOWED SAME. A REPORT IS FILED #333210. EXPLAINING WHAT HAPPEND AFTER.

201

38 1 White to Records Section Pink To Assigned Bureau Yellow To Investigating Officer

CRIME REPORT
POLICE DIVISION
TOLEDO, OHIO
Form 38.1 Rev 8/81
JUVENILE ☐

SPECIAL	1 VICTIM Last, First, Middle (Firm Name if Business)	DILLION JIMI D.
Warrant	2 Records Section No.	33321C
Bar		

3 TYPE OF CRIME	4 Location of Occurrence
CRIMINAL DAMAGE	WASHINGTON + ERIE

6 UCR Code and Number	7 Type of Premises or Name of Business Where Offense Was Committed	8 Beat
26-557	PUBLIC STREET	

ROUTING
ADMIN.
Inspections
Internal Aff.
Off. Of Chief
ADMIN. SER.
Crime Preven.
Comm. Rel.
Training
Personnel
INVEST. SER.
Crimes/Person
Crimes/Prop
Youth Ser.
Vice/Narcotic
FIELD OPER.
Patrol
Traffic
SUPP. SER.
Communn.
Prop. Mgt.
OTHER
Fire
Law

9 Date and Time Occurred	10 Day of Week	11 Date and Time Reported
5-23-83 2045	MON	5-23-83 2100

12 Reporting Person's Name (Last, First, Middle)	13 Victim's Race	Sex	Age	D.O.B	Occupation
I.I.	B	M	34	12-12-48	SEC. GUARD

14 Reporting Person's Residence Address	15 Res. Phone	16 Victim's Residence Address	City	17 Res. Phone
		132 PAGE	TOL	255-0669

18 Reporting Person's Business Address	19 Bus. Phone	20 Victim's Business Address	21 Bus. Phone
		5741937 W. ALEXIS SUITE 1	474-52C

22 WITNESS NO. 1 - NAME (Last, First, Middle)	Age	Residence Address	City	Res. Phone	Bus. Phone
NESBITT, ROSIE M	22	1113 CAMPBELL	TOL	244-6866	
WITNESS NO. 2 - NAME (Last, First, Middle)	Age	Residence Address	City	Res. Phone	Bus. Phone

23 Color	Year	Make	Model	Style	License No. (State, Year)	V.I.N	Towed Where?
GRN	70	CHEVY	CAMERO	2DR	DXZ 565		

Registered Owner's Name	Registered Owner's Residence Address	☐ HOLDER
SAME -		☐ Suspect's ☐ Victim's

24 SUSPECT NO. 1 - NAME (Last, First, Middle)	25 Race	26 Sex	27 Age	28 D.O.B	29 Hgt.	30 Weight	31 Hair	32 Eyes

33 Address (Apt. No.)	Phone	City	34 Date and Time of Arrest	35 Advised of Rights? Yes __ No __

36 Clothing and Other Identifiers	37 B.I.R. No.	38 Arrest Number

SUSPECT NO. 2 - NAME (Last, First, Middle)	25 Race	26 Sex	27 Age	28 D.O.B	29 Hgt.	30 Weight	31 Hair	32 Eyes

333210	ADDRESS (Apt. No.)	Phone	City	34 Date and Time of Arrest	35 Advised of Rights? Yes __ No __
	Clothing and Other Identifiers		37 B.I.R. No.	38 Arrest Number	

39 CRIMES AGAINST PROPERTY - Point Where Entrance Was Made	40 Exact Location of Property When Stolen
☒ Force ☐ No Force ☐ Attempt	NOTHING STOLEN -

41 Instrument Used (Describe)	42 Method Used to Gain Entrance
BROOM HANDLE -	NO ENTRANCE

43 Where Was Occupant At Time of Entrance	44 Trademark of Suspect - Action or Conversation
INSIDE IN VEH. STOPPED AT A RED LIGHT.	HOLLERED "NIGGER YOU AIN'T SEEN NOTHIN YET"

45 CRIMES AGAINST PERSON - Weapon, Force, or Means Used	46 Exact Location of Victim at Time of Offense
☐ Weapon ☐ Strongarm (No Weapon)	

47 Victim's Activity at Time of Offense	48 Apparent Motive - Type of Property Taken or Obtained

49 EXACT Words Used By Suspect(s)

50 TYPE OF NARCOTIC	51 Dictated for Transcription?
☐ Heroin, Morphine ☐ Cocaine, Opium ☐ Marijuana, Hashish ☐ Synthetic Narcotics ☐ LSD, PCP, Benzedrine ☐ Inhalents ☐ Possession of Implements ☐ Forging of Prescriptions	Yes __ No __
	52 Follow-up Required? Yes ☐ No ☒

53 TYPE OF GAMBLING	54 ARREST ON:
☐ Bookmaking (Horses, Sports) ☐ Numbers, Lottery ☐ Cards, Dice, Pool, All Others ☐ Bingo	☐ Warrant ☐ Attachment ☐ View

55 WEAPON:	Describe Weapon	56 INDICATE
☐ Gun ☐ Knife ☐ Hands/Feet ☒ Other	BROOM HANDLE	☐ Yard Search ☐ Detective Notified ☐ Field Search ☐ Detective on Scene ☐ Area Search ☐ Evid. Tech. on Scene ☐ Cursory ☐ Intensive ☐ Summons

57 PREMISES TYPE	POINT OF ENTRY & LOCATION	METHOD USED
1 Residence	8 Medical	20 Door 25 Front	40 Open/Unlocked
2 Apt/Duplex	9 Office Bldg.	21 Window 26 Rear	41 Body Force
3 Hotel/Motel	10 Manufacturer	22 Garage Door 27 Side	42 Pry/Cutting
4 School	11 Gas Station	23 Adjacent Premises 28 Roof	43 Channel Locks
5 Church	12 Chain Store	24 Other 29 Other	44 Break Glass
6 Bar/Restaurant	13 Small Business		
7 Bank	14 Highway/Street	(Describe Other)	

TAB N.C

58	Street Index	Property	M.O. Index	Tab

59 Report Made By	Officer(s) Name(s)	I.D. No.	Unit No.	60 Officer Assigned to Case	61 Supervisor's Approval
SHEILA	JOHNSON	564	REC-6		

62 DISPOSITION				202		
☐ UNFOUNDED	☐ CLEARED-NO ARREST	☐ CLEARED BY ARREST	☐ ADJUSTED	☐ INVESTIGATION CONTINUES	☐ INACTIVE CASE

White to Records Section, Pink To Assigned Bureau, Yellow To Investigating Officer

DILLON JIMI. D' |CRIMINAL DAMAGE| WASHINGTON + ERIE | 333210

64	Quantity	PROPERTY ☐ TAKEN ☐ RECOVERED (List) Name, Brand, Model, Color, Size, Type, License Number		Serial Number	Value
				Total Value Loss $	

65 EVIDENCE Where Found, By Whom, Disposition

Evidence Preserved At Scene
a ☐ Possible Fingerprints   c ☐ Body Fluids
b ☐ Footprints   d ☐ Tool Marks

Disposition of Evidence Removed From Scene (Marked & Tagged)
e ☐ Booked/Property Room   g ☐ Investigative Safe
f ☐ Night Property Room   h ☐ District Station Property
☐ Flammable   ☐ Stor Cab.   Property Number

66 DETAILS. (Address the categories listed below, where applicable, in the order they appear.)
(1) List additional victims.   (2) List additional witnesses.   (3) List additional suspects, descriptions, arrestees, charges
(4) If Juvenile involved as victim or suspect, list parents' names (last, first, middle), phone number, school attended, and whether parents notified
(5) If victim injured, describe injuries and where treated.
(6) Indicate time and location where victims and witnesses may be contacted later for follow-up.
(7) Indicate if victim, reporting person, witness or suspect gave statement. Record statement on Supplemental Report, if necessary.
(8) Itemize additional property taken, giving name, brand, model, serial no., caliber of guns, identifying marks, and value of each item.
(9) List additional physical evidence, where found, by whom, disposition, and identifying marks.
(10) Provide additional description on vehicle (unusual paint, body, marks, or damage). Describe additional vehicles.
(11) If vehicle stolen, give Title number and value. Car unlocked, keys in ignition? List name of insurance and/or finance company
(12) Reconstruct the incident - include all necessary elements of the crime

(12) VICTIM + WITNESS #1 WERE STOPPED AT A RED LIGHT ON ERIE AT WASHINGTON WHEN A GROUP OF WHITE MALES (4) IN A GRAY + BLACK ~~CUTLASS~~ FIREBIRD WITH LICENCE PLATE. OH. ANC748. JUMPED OUT AND HOLLERED "NIGGER YOU AIN'T SEEN NOTHING YET," AND THEN ~~SMA~~ THE DRIVER GOT OUT AND SMASHED OUT VICTIM'S BACK WINDOW. VICTIM WISHES TO PROSECUTE SUSPECT FOR CRIMINAL DAMAGE. DONE TO HIS VEHICLE. OH LIC. ANC 748 IS REGISTERED TO KENNETH S. SMITH, 740 WALBRIDGE, TOLEDO OH ON A 1979 PONTIAC.

203

#27

In certain cultures some people have been engulfed with calamity and never overcome. Yet others have overcome and lived to tell their story, even as Job did in the Holy Bible, and the boy's case is no exception to this fact. Now you have met Lablekgahe Yankpund, Nahee, Daniel, the boy, and Jimi—all referring to the author. In spite of his calamities, the boy exclaims in the words of Maya Anagelou "But still I rise."

www.ingramcontent.com/pod-product-compliance
Lightning Source LLC
Chambersburg PA
CBHW051413280526
4578SCB00003B/1052